THE LAW COMMISSION  KU-281-444

Working Paper No.113

FAMILY LAW

DOMESTIC VIOLENCE AND OCCUPATION OF

THE FAMILY HOME

TABLE OF CONTENTS

LONDON
HER MAJESTY'S STATIONERY OFFICE

© Crown copyright 1989
First published 1989

ISBN 0 11 730195 7

THE LAW COMMISSION

WORKING PAPER NO. 113

FAMILY LAW

DOMESTIC VIOLENCE AND OCCUPATION OF
THE FAMILY HOME

SUMMARY

In this consultative paper the Law Commission examines the
remedies provided by family law relating to occupation of the family
home and protection of family members from domestic violence and other
forms of molestation. The paper does not review either the criminal
law sanctions or housing law remedies sometimes available in cases of
domestic violence and relationship breakdown.

The paper details the various criticisms which may be made of
the existing remedies and makes particular proposals for reform. No
fundamental change in the present system is suggested but a scheme
designed to show how a unified structure of remedies might look is put
forward.

THE LAW COMMISSION

WORKING PAPER NO.113

FAMILY LAW

DOMESTIC VIOLENCE AND OCCUPATION OF
THE FAMILY HOME

PART I

INTRODUCTION

1.1   The aim of this paper is to review the various discretionary
remedies which have been provided or developed within family law for
dealing with two inter-related problems: first the occupation of the
family home, and secondly, protection of one family member against
molestation or violence by another.

1.2   It is not our aim to review the whole of the law relating to
domestic violence.[1] Most acts of violence are also crimes, but the
object of the criminal law is primarily to punish and deter the
offender, whereas the object of family law is primarily to protect the
victim. Similarly, it is not our aim to review the obligations of
housing authorities and others to provide alternative accommodation
when family relationships break down.[2] The inter-relationship between

---

[1.] The Commission is at present reviewing the law on binding over,
which is also relevant in Domestic disputes; see Binding Over: The
Issues (1987), Working Paper No. 103, paras. 7.8-7.12.

[2.] A Department of the Environment Working Party is currently
considering the extent of the problem of relationship breakdown and
public sector housing.

1

the remedies available to family members and the legal position of third parties, such as landlords and mortgagees, is obviously relevant to a review of the former but it is not our intention to propose any significant alteration in the latter.[3]

1.3   This review is undertaken as part of the "comprehensive examination of family law... with a view to its systematic reform and eventual codification" required under Item XIX of our Second Programme of Law Reform.[4] The time is particularly ripe for such a review. The Children Bill now before Parliament provides, not only for a single set of remedies relating to the care and upbringing of children to be available in all courts and in all proceedings, but also for concurrent jurisdiction in the High Court, county courts and magistrates' courts, with powers of vertical and horizontal transfer between them.[5] Our aim is therefore two-fold: first, to see whether the existing remedies can be improved, and secondly, to consider how far they might synthesised into a single set of remedies which could be made available in all courts and all family proceedings.

1.4   Three statutes give express power to grant non-molestation or ouster type orders. Under the Matrimonial Homes Act 1983,[6] the High Court and county courts may make a variety of orders enforcing or restricting the respective rights of spouses to occupy their

---

[3.] See particularly paras. 6.5-6.7 and 6.50-6.53 below.

[4.] Second Programme of Law Reform (1968), Law Com. No.14.

[5.] Children Bill [as amended in Standing Committee B], clause 82, is a "marker" for a more comprehensive provision to be tabled later; for the Government's intentions, see Hansard (H.L.), 6 December 1988, Vol.505, cols.494-495; Hansard (H.C.), 27 April 1989, Vol.151, cols. 1115, 1182; Official Report (H.C.), Standing Committee B, 8 June 1989, cols.456 et seq.

[6.] Consolidating the Matrimonial Homes Act 1967 with later amendments.

matrimonial home.[7]   The Domestic Violence and Matrimonial Proceedings Act 1976 empowers county courts to grant injunctions against molestation or excluding one party from the home, in respect not only of married couples but also of partners who are living together as husband and wife.[8] Finally, the Domestic Proceedings and Magistrates' Courts Act 1978 empowers magistrates' courts to make orders protecting one spouse against violence by the other, including the power to exclude a violent spouse from the home.[9] Magistrates' powers therefore apply only to the use or threat of violence and only between married partners.

1.5   Preceding the introduction of these specific statutory powers, and now co-existing with them, are the general powers of the High Court and county courts to grant injunctions.[10]   These are either ancillary to some other remedy within the court's jurisdiction or in support of a right recognised by the general law.   Thus, for many years divorce courts have granted injunctions prohibiting molestation when proceedings for divorce, nullity or judicial separation are pending, sometimes also controlling the parties' occupation of the matrimonial home. Similarly, where the protection of a minor is at issue, injunctions may be granted in wardship or ancillary to claims for custody under the Guardianship of Minors Act 1971.   Injunctions may also be granted to protect victims from the torts of assault and battery or trespass to land or otherwise in support of property rights recognised under the general law.   Magistrates' courts have no

---

7. ss.1(2) and 9(1). Unless a proprietary right exists, or the court has ordered otherwise, a spouse's personal right of occupation comes to an end on dissolution of the marriage.

8. s.1(1) and (2).

9. s.16(2) and (3).

10. In the High Court, under the Supreme Court Act 1981, s.37. By the County Courts Act 1984, s.38, a county court, as regards any cause of action within its jurisdiction, has the same power as the High Court to grant an injunction.

jurisdiction in matters of property or tort, nor do they have any power to grant injunctions.[11]

1.6   The discrepancies between the remedies themselves and between the powers of different courts have prompted complaints about the complexity as well as the effectiveness of the civil law in relation to domestic violence.[12]   Powers to oust one party or mandatory injunctions allowing return to the matrimonial home are inextricably linked with both short-term occupation rights and the provision of long-term accommodation. However, as Lord Scarman has observed:

"The statutory provision is a hotchpotch of enactments of limited scope passed into law to meet specific situations or to strengthen the powers of the specified courts. The sooner the range, scope, and effect of these powers are rationalised into a coherent and comprehensive body of statute law, the better".[13]

1.7   The problems of devising such a scheme in the present context are considerable. First, there is the complex inter-relationship between the statutory remedies developed within family law and the ordinary law of property and tort. Secondly, there are the difficulties of accommodating the magistrates' powers within such a structure. Thirdly, and most importantly of all, the family law remedies have themselves been developed to meet a variety of needs. Some were specifically devised to deal with the problem of domestic violence, and other forms of molestation, where protection of the

---

11. Thus an injunction might be granted in connection with a Guardianship of Minors Act case in the High Court or a county court but not in a magistrates' court.

12. E.g. Women's National Commission, Violence against Women, Report of an ad hoc Working Group (1985); L. Smith, Domestic Violence: an overview of the literature, Home Office Research Study No. 107 (1989).

13. Richards v. Richards [1984] A.C. 174, 206-7.

4

person is the predominant purpose. Others were originally devised to secure the right to occupy the family home in the short or longer term, but have since been developed to include a power to oust one party in the interests of the other. The principles applicable in one context are not necessarily appropriate in the other. Nevertheless, the two cannot be treated separately because, so frequently, the only effective protection against family violence or molestation is the removal of one party from the home.

1.8   In Part II of this paper we give a brief account of the development of the existing law. In Parts III, IV and V we analyse and compare the details of various remedies available and the criticisms which may be made of them. In Part VI we discuss possible approaches to reform. Appendix A outlines a possible scheme for ouster orders in child protection cases and Appendix B contains a "checklist" of the specific proposals upon which we would welcome views.

PART II

BACKGROUND

2.1   In this Part we trace the development of the various remedies now available, in roughly the chronological order in which they appeared. A recurring theme, however, is how a remedy developed for a particular purpose in one context has later been adopted or adapted for different purposes in another.

Injunctions issued ancillary to matrimonial proceedings

2.2   The principles relating to the grant of injunctions against molestation or excluding a spouse from the matrimonial home were first evolved by the courts in considering applications made ancillary to proceedings for divorce, judicial separation or nullity.[1] While matrimonial proceedings are pending a spouse has the right to pursue remedies in the courts free from threats, intimidation or coercion. If such interference were found, the courts would assist by ensuring that the victimised spouse was not prevented from pursuing the action. Initially the intervention of the court included the grant of an injunction to exclude the husband from the matrimonial home, provided that the husband's conduct complained of made it "impossible" for her to live in the house while he was living there too.[2] It was therefore in this context that the advantages of ouster injunctions as an effective protection against domestic violence first became apparent.[3]

---

[1] E.g. in Silverstone v. Silverstone [1953] P. 174, Pearce J. held that the divorce court had power to restrain a husband from entering the matrimonial home pending the hearing of his wife's petition, even though he was the owner of the premises.

[2] Ibid., see also Hall v. Hall [1971] 1 W.L.R. 404.

[3] See particularly S. Maidment, "The Law's Response to Marital Violence In England and the U.S.A." (1977) 26 I.C.L.Q. 403.

Later case law placed less emphasis on blame and concentrated more on the issue of what in the circumstances, was fair, just and reasonable. Frequently on the facts of those cases the children's interests were found to be the deciding factor.[4]

2.3   In accordance with the general rule that an injunction will only be granted to support a legal right,[5] the majority of matrimonial injunctions were obtained ancillary to proceedings for divorce. Although it was clear that if proceedings for divorce were pending there was a sufficient nexus between the petition and the protection sought, it was not clear what other proceedings must be pending before the court had jurisdiction to grant injunctive relief. In particular, it might be necessary to distinguish between injunctions against violence and other forms of molestation, which might be justified either by the need to protect litigants or by the general law of tort, and injunctions excluding one party from the home, which might depend upon their respective claims to occupy it.[6]

Rights of occupation

2.4   At common law the contract of marriage imposes a mutual obligation on spouses to live together.   Flowing from this is the right of each spouse to share in the occupation of the matrimonial

---

[4.] See e.g. Stewart v. Stewart [1973] Fam. 21; Phillips v. Phillips [1973] 1 W.L.R 615; Bassett v. Bassett [1975] Fam. 76; Walker v. Walker [1978] 1 W.L.R. 533; cf. now paras. 3.6 et seq. below.

[5.] North London Railway Co. v. Great Northern Railway Co. (1883) 11 Q.B.D. 30; Montgomery v. Montgomery [1965] P. 46.

[6.] In Winstone v. Winstone [1960] P. 28, it was found that there was not sufficient nexus between an application for leave to petition for divorce and an injunction excluding the respondent husband from the matrimonial home. Cf. McGibbon v. McGibbon [1973] Fam. 170, where a non-molestation injunction was granted on similar facts because of the risk of the applicant being bullied out of her rights.

home irrespective of ownership. At common law this right could be lost by matrimonial misconduct. Further, in National Provincial Bank Ltd. v. Ainsworth,[7] it was held to be a personal rather than a proprietary right which therefore could not bind third parties to whom the owning spouse had transferred or mortgaged the property. However, where the property was held on a protected or statutory tenancy under the Rent Acts, the fact that the tenant spouse was unable to evict the other meant that the landlord would be unable to obtain possession of the premises unless a statutory ground for doing so (such as non-payment of rent) arose.[8]

2.5   Since 1967 the non-entitled spouse has also enjoyed statutory rights of occupation under the Matrimonial Homes Act. The 1967 Act was principally passed to reverse the House of Lords' decision in National Provincial Bank Ltd. v. Ainsworth.[9] Its main purpose was therefore to turn the personal right of occupation enjoyed by the non-owning spouse into a land charge which could be protected by registration against dispositions to third parties by the owning spouse. Further, recognising the practical inability of the landlord to evict the spouse of a Rent Act tenant once payments by the occupier counted as rent, it provided a new power in the courts to transfer such tenancies from one to the other when the parties divorced.[10]

---

7. [1965] A.C. 1175.

8. Brown v. Draper [1944] K.B. 309; Middleton v. Baldock [1950] 1 K.B. 657; Old Gate Estates Ltd. v. Alexander [1950] 1 K.B. 311. The tenure of the occupying spouse could well be insecure, however, because the tenant might cease to pay the rent and the landlord did not have to accept payment from the occupier. This has now been rectified by the Matrimonial Homes Act 1983, s.1(5).

9. [1965] A.C. 1175.

10. Now contained in the Matrimonial Homes Act 1983, s.7 and Sched.1; since extended to assured tenancies by the Housing Act 1988 and secure local authority tenancies by the Housing Act 1980 (now 1985).

2.6   Of equal importance in the long run, however, have been the powers given by the Matrimonial Homes Act to regulate and adjust the respective rights of occupation between the spouses themselves. Originally, the courts had power to uphold or to end the occupation rights of a non-owning spouse but it was held in Tarr v. Tarr[11] that the 1967 Act gave no power to exclude the legal owner altogether. This again was remedied by the Domestic Violence and Matrimonial Proceedings Act 1976, which also introduced a new power to adjust the occupation rights of spouses who were joint owners or tenants.[12] Since then, the legislation has provided that either of the spouses may apply to the court for an order:-

> - declaring, enforcing, restricting or terminating the rights of occupation of a non-owning spouse;
> - prohibiting, suspending or restricting the exercise by either spouse of the right to occupy the dwelling house; or
> - requiring either spouse to permit the exercise by the other of that right.[13]

2.7   The Matrimonial Homes Act has taken on new significance since the decision of the House of Lords in Richards v. Richards, where it was held that the effect of the Act was to:

> "codify and spell out... the jurisdiction of the High Court and the county court in ouster injunctions between spouses whether in pending proceedings or by way of originating summons."[14]

---

11. [1973] A.C. 254.

12. The Matrimonial Homes Act 1967 as amended by the Domestic Violence and Matrimonial Proceedings Act 1976, ss.3 and 4, now consolidated in the Matrimonial Homes Act 1983.

13. Matrimonial Homes Act 1983, ss.1(2), and 9(1).

14. Richards v. Richards [1984] A.C.174, 202 per Lord Hailsham.

This means that the factors indicated in section 1(3) of the Matrimonial Homes Act[15] are to be regarded as the universal criteria for deciding applications which seek to oust one party from the home. Before Richards v. Richards the Matrimonial Homes Act was not extensively used at all.[16] It was not passed to provide a remedy for a wife threatened with violence but to ensure that any deserving spouse had a roof over her head.[17] Until 1976, it did not provide for an owning spouse to be excluded. Nor is there any express power to protect against molestation before or after the hearing. The provisions of the Matrimonial Homes Act could never be said to have been designed for those women, popularly named "battered wives", on whose plight public concern was focusing in the early 1970's.

Actions in tort

2.8   An action between spouses in tort became possible in 1962, but the jurisdiction is ultimately a discretionary one. The Law Reform (Husband and Wife) Act 1962 provides that each spouse has the same right of action against the other in tort as if they were not married.[18]   However, this is subject to the court's discretion to stay an action if it appears that no substantial benefit would accrue

---

15. See para. 3.8 below.

16. In 1982 there were only 53 applications in the county courts for such orders whereas there were 26,428 applications for injunctions ancillary to divorce proceedings (not all of which were ousters) and 7,691 applications under s.1 Domestic Violence and Matrimonial Proceedings Act 1976. Judicial Statistics Annual Report (1982) Table 4.8.

17. Report on Matrimonial Proceedings in Magistrates' Courts (1976), Law Com. No. 77, para. 3.27.

18. The rule that husband and wife could not sue each other in tort was one of the last vestiges of the common law's doctrine that they were one person in law. It survived the Married Women's Property Act 1882, which stripped the husband of control over the wife's property.

to either party from the continuation of the proceedings.[19] This discretion retains the possibility of discrimination on the sole basis of the parties' marital status.

2.9   As between spouses, there was little need to resort to tort law, because matrimonial remedies were available.   As between cohabitants and other family members however, an action in tort might be the only way to proceed.   This is not wholly appropriate in the context of domestic violence because the main object of the tort system is financial compensation and in most cases this will either not be available or will reduce the resources otherwise used to maintain the family.   Injunctions can nonetheless be effective remedies for the torts of assault, battery, nuisance or trespass.[20] In the High Court, such injunctions might be the only relief claimed, whereas in county courts they have generally to be ancillary to a claim for damages or some other cause or matter within the court's jurisdiction.

The Domestic Violence and Matrimonial Proceedings Act 1976

2.10   In February 1975 a Select Committee was appointed to consider the extent, nature and causes of problems of families where there is violence between the partners or where children suffer non-accidental injury.   The committee concentrated on the "battered wife" aspect of its terms of reference, women, that is:

---

19. Law Reform (Husband and Wife) Act 1962, s.1(2)(a).

20. E.g. Egan v. Egan [1975] Ch. 218, where the plaintiff mother suffered continual physical assaults at the hands of her 19 year old son. Oliver J. granted an interlocutory injunction restraining the respondent's continued trespass on her property after his licence had been withdrawn and from "assaulting, molesting, annoying or otherwise interfering with the plaintiff".   But see now Patel v. Patel [1988] 2 F.L.R. 179, paras. 4.12-4.13 below, for the proper scope of such injunctions, given that there is no general tort of harassment in English law.

"[who] are often with inadequate means and with dependent children, and in need of shelter or help or advice for themselves and their families."[21]

While admitting that no laws, however well enforced, could prevent marital assaults, the Select Committee made a number of recommendations for new powers to be applied in all courts. Jo Richardson M.P. introduced a private Member's Bill which became the Domestic Violence and Matrimonial Proceedings Act 1976. It was said, by Lord Salmon, to have been:

"hurried through Parliament to provide urgently needed first aid for 'battered wives'."[22]

2.11 The new provisions overcame the lack of jurisdiction that had previously prevented a county court from granting an injunction unless it could be shown to be incidental to other proceedings. It gave jurisdiction to all county courts to grant the following types of injunction whether or not there were other proceedings before the court:-

- restraining the other party to the marriage from molesting the applicant;
- restraining the other party from molesting a child living with the applicant;
- excluding the other party from the matrimonial home or a part of the matrimonial home or from a specified area in which the matrimonial home is included;

---

21. Report from the Select Committee on Violence in Marriage (1974-75), HC 553-i, Vol.1. para.6.

22. Davis v. Johnson [1979] A.C. 264, 340.

- requiring the other party to permit the applicant to enter and remain in the matrimonial home or a part of the matrimonial home.[23]

These powers were to apply both between parties to a marriage and between "a man and woman who are living with each other in the same household as husband and wife".[24]

2.12   Initially it was thought that section 1 of the 1976 Act was only a procedural provision overcoming the previous limitations on the county courts' powers.   It was not thought to have altered the substantive law so as to enable the court to override common law property rights.[25] However, in Davis v. Johnson,[26] the House of Lords held, by a majority of 4 to 1, that section 1 of the Act did give a county court jurisdiction to exclude both a spouse and, as in this case, a cohabitant from the matrimonial home irrespective of any right of property vested in the person excluded whether he be the sole or joint owner or tenant.[27]   Section 1, however, can only give temporary relief and its purpose is not to affect existing property rights but to override or interfere with the enjoyment of such rights.   As Lord Scarman explained,

---

23. The 1976 Act, s.1(1).

24. s.1(2); references to the "matrimonial" home are to be construed accordingly.

25. See e.g. B. v. B. [1978] 1 All E.R. 821; Cantliff v. Jenkins [1978] Q.B. 47.

26. Davis v. Johnson [1979] A.C. 264.

27. In this case the applicant was a joint tenant with her cohabitant partner and therefore had a legal right to continue in peaceful occupation of the premises in which she had been living. Lord Diplock would have confined the decision to such joint tenants.

"the purpose of the section is not to create rights but to strengthen remedies."[28]

2.13 Taking note of the heartfelt complaints made by many women that, because of the slow enforcement procedures, civil injunctions were not worth the paper they were written on, the Select Committee had also recommended that the courts have power to attach a police power of arrest to injunctions. This recommendation was implemented by section 2 of the Domestic Violence and Matrimonial Proceedings Act 1976. This applies to all injunctions restraining violence or excluding one party from the home, whatever the proceedings in which they were granted, but as with section 1, only between spouses or people living together as such.[29]

Jurisdiction of the magistrates' courts

2.14 The matrimonial jurisdiction of the magistrates' courts evolved in response to a particular concern about the position of working class women who suffered repeated physical assaults from their husbands.[30] In 1878 the Matrimonial Causes Act gave magistrates' courts the power to grant a separation order, with maintenance and custody of children under ten, to a wife whose husband had been convicted of an aggravated assault on her, "if satisfied that the future safety of the wife (was) in peril."[31] The separation order had

---

28. Davis v. Johnson [1979] A.C. 264, 349.

29. Cf. Re G. (Wardship)(Jurisdiction: Power of Arrest) (1983) 4 F.L.R. 538: there is no inherent power in wardship to attach a power of arrest to an injunction against a father who has never lived with or been married to the mother.

30. See Report of the Committee of One-Parent Families (the Finer Report) (1974), Cmnd. 5629, Vol.1, para. 4.67 and O.R. McGregor, Divorce in England, (1957), Ch.1.

31. The Matrimonial Causes Act 1878, s.4. The proviso was removed by the Summary Jurisdiction (Married Women) Act 1895.

14

the force and effect of a decree of judicial separation on the ground of cruelty.[32] Except in so far as the award of maintenance provided wives with a limited financial means of escape,[33] the award of a separation order did little else to ensure personal safety.

2.15   The 1978 Act abolished the separation order and provided new remedies specifically designed to protect a spouse, usually the wife, or child from a violent and dangerous husband within the matrimonial home.   The general objects of the Act were stated by the Law Commission, in its Report on Matrimonial Proceedings in Magistrates' Courts, to be twofold:-

- to bring the family law administered by the magistrates' courts into line with the law administered by the divorce courts; and
-to introduce such changes as were called for in order to avoid the creation of anomalies.[34]

Two new remedies were created:

"the personal protection order which will merely prohibit him (the husband) from behaving in a way which is dangerous to his wife and children (and) the exclusion order... which will have the positive and drastic result of preventing the husband from living in his own home".[35]

---

32. Ibid.

33. Maintenance orders were frequently for derisory sums and irregularly paid. See Finer Report (1974), Cmnd. 5629, Vol.1. paras. 4.87-4.101.

34. (1976), Law Com. No.77. para. 1.1

35. Ibid., para. 3.18.

These powers are quite independent of any other claim, for example to financial relief, and either party may apply. The court may also attach a power of arrest to an order.[36] These powers are essentially emergency measures and were not intended to resolve long term occupation rights between spouses.[37]

Other potential jurisdictions

2.16   The Domestic Violence and Matrimonial Proceedings Act 1976 gave a county court the same powers as had the High Court to grant injunctions even though no other relief was sought. However, injunctions are still sought both in pending matrimonial proceedings and in actions in tort and the general law of property. The general power of the High Court to grant both final and interlocutory injunctions, "in all cases in which it appears to the court to be just and convenient to do so", has statutory basis in section 37 Supreme Court Act 1981.[38] The general rule is that an injunction will only be granted to support a legal right.[39] Any legal or equitable right may therefore be protected by an injunction providing that the injunction bears some relation to the substantive suit.[40]

---

36. Domestic Proceedings and Magistrates' Courts Act 1978, s.18. This power did not feature in the original Bill.

37. (1976), Law Com. No.77., paras. 3.26 - 3.27.

38. According to Lord Hailsham in Richards v. Richards [1984] A.C. 174, 199 any inherent power available to the High Court was absorbed by the statutory provisions. Also see County Courts Act 1984, s.38, for similar powers relating to matters within the jurisdiction of the county courts.

39. North London Railway Co. v. Great Northern Railway Co. (1883) 11 Q.B.D. 30.

40. Des Salles d'Epinoix v. Des Salles d'Epinoix [1967] 1 W.L.R. 553.

2.17   Abuse or violence directed at a spouse or cohabitant will also
affect children living in the home, who, because of their intimate
contact, may also be at risk of either emotional or physical harm.
The Domestic Violence and Matrimonial Proceedings Act 1976 and the
Domestic Proceedings and Magistrates Court Act 1978, enable a spouse
(and, in the first, a cohabitant) to apply for protection for "a child
living with the applicant"[41] and "a child of the family"[42]
respectively.   The courts' general powers to grant interlocutory
injunctions [43] have been used in the course of custody proceedings
under the Guardianship of Minors Act 1971[44] and wardship proceedings
in the High Court.[45] The general law of tort has also been called in
aid to protect other family members from assault, destruction of
property, menacing, and fear within, and unwarranted exclusion from,
the matrimonial or family home.[46]

[41.] Domestic Violence and Matrimonial Proceedings Act 1976, s.1.

[42.] Domestic Proceedings and Magistrates' Courts Act 1978, s.16.

[43.] Re W. (A Minor) [1981] 3 All E.R. 401, 403 per Lord Brandon.

[44.] See Re W. (A Minor) [1981] 3 All E.R. 401 where both a
non-molestation and ouster order were granted in the county court
as ancillary to a custody order under the Guardianship of Minors
Act 1971 but cf. paras. 4.14 et seq. below.

[45.] Re V. (A Minor)(Wardship) (1979) 123 S.J. 201; cf. Re T.(A Minor:
Wardship; T. v. T. (Ouster Order) [1987] 1 F.L.R. 181.

[46.] E.g. Egan v. Egan [1975] 1 Ch. 218, (molestation of mother by
son); Bush v. Green [1985] 1 W.L.R. 1143, (former cohabitant
stripped the contents of the family home which was held in their
joint names); Tabone v. Seguna [1986] 1 F.L.R. 591 (molestation of
mother and daughter by man living with another daughter); Smith v.
Smith [1988] 1 F.L.R. 179 (molestation by former cohabitant).

PART III

REMEDIES, SCOPE AND CRITERIA

3.1   The remedies with which we are here concerned are the statutory powers under the Matrimonial Homes Act 1983, the Domestic Violence and Matrimonial Proceedings Act 1976, and the Domestic Proceedings and Magistrates' Courts Act 1978, together with the power to grant similar remedies in divorce or other family proceedings. In this Part, we examine the scope of the relief available under each, the criteria governing the exercise of the courts' discretion, and the potential duration of orders.

The scope of occupation, ouster or exclusion orders

3.2   Under the Matrimonial Homes Act 1983, the court has power to make orders "prohibiting, suspending or restricting the right of either spouse to occupy" the matrimonial home or "requiring either spouse to permit the exercise by the other of that right".[1] Where only one of them is legally entitled to the home there is also power to make an order "declaring, enforcing, restricting or terminating" the statutory rights of occupation of the non-entitled spouse.[2] Orders to the effect that one spouse should leave the home are not technically termed injunctions but the effect is the same. The Act also gives power to make ancillary orders as to the discharge of outgoings, repairs and maintenance by either spouse; to except part of the house from the non-entitled spouse's rights; and to order a non-entitled spouse to pay for occupation.[3]

[1.] ss.1(2)(b) and (c) and 9(1).

[2.] s.1(2)(a).

[3.] s.1(3).

3.3   Section 1 of the Domestic Violence and Matrimonial Proceedings Act 1976 gives power to grant injunctions "excluding the other party from the matrimonial home or a part of the matrimonial home or from a specified area in which the matrimonial home is included" or "requiring the other party to permit the applicant to enter or remain in the matrimonial home".[4]   These are much the same as the orders which are made in pending divorce proceedings, where, for example, each spouse might be restricted to a particular part of the house or one spouse excluded from the block, the street or indeed a wider area in which the matrimonial home is situated.   In practice, considerable care may be taken to tailor the precise terms of the order to the circumstances of the particular case.   It is not uncommon, for example, to permit the respondent to return for the purposes of visiting his children, conducting a trade or business, or collecting personal property.   To this extent these powers are wider than those in the Matrimonial Homes Act.   There is, however, no power to make ancillary orders about the discharge of outgoings or payment for occupation, although this can sometimes be dealt with by undertakings.

3.4   The Domestic Proceedings and Magistrates' Courts Act 1978 gives magistrates' courts power to exclude one spouse from the home and at the same time (but not otherwise) to order the excluded spouse to allow the other spouse to enter and remain there.[5]   The order may be subject to "exceptions or conditions";[6] the scope of this is not entirely plain but it may allow conditions as to outgoings or payment for occupation, or restriction to part of the home.   It could perhaps allow for conditions prohibiting the respondent from removing or damaging the furniture which is not provided for under the other

---

[4]. s.1(1)(c) and (d).

[5]. s.16(3) and (4).

[6]. s.16(9).

legislation.[7] There is no power to exclude from a wider area and in practice it may be more difficult to tailor the precise terms of the order to the circumstances of the individual case.

3.5   One issue for consideration, therefore, is whether these discrepancies might be removed, thus allowing all courts to deal flexibly with the possibility that both parties may continue in the home, at some times or for some purposes; to exclude one of them from a wider area than the home itself; and to make consequential orders about outgoings. Many orders are granted in the first instance on short notice, or even ex parte, when it will be impracticable to inquire into the financial implications at that stage. Nevertheless, as we shall see,[8] some are made in circumstances or for a period during which such powers could well be useful.

Criteria for ouster or exclusion orders

3.6   The general powers under which the courts grant injunctions in pending proceedings refer simply to what is "just and convenient".[9] Neither they nor section 1 of the 1976 Act, which makes no reference to violence, lay down any criteria for the exercise of the courts' discretion. Before the House of Lords' decision in Richards v. Richards,[10] therefore, the courts had developed their own principles, in which the relative hardship to the parties and the interests of their children played the largest part.[11] Eventually, however, there

---

[7]. Davis v. Johnson [1979] A.C. 264, the man excluded for serious violence sent some of his friends to remove all the furniture from the flat.

[8]. See paras. 3.32 et seq. below.

[9]. Supreme Court Act 1981, s.37; County Courts Act 1984, s.38.

[10]. [1984] A.C.174.

[11]. E.g. Bassett v. Bassett [1975] Fam. 76; Walker v. Walker [1978] 1 W.L.R. 533.

were conflicting decisions in the Court of Appeal on the weight to be
given to the reason why the applicant found it impossible to continue
under the same roof pending divorce proceedings.[12]

3.7   The House of Lords in Richards v. Richards[13] decided that
where an ouster injunction is sought between spouses, whether in
pending matrimonial proceedings or under the Domestic Violence and
Matrimonial Proceedings Act 1976, the application is now to be viewed
as a procedure whereby either spouse might establish, and enforce by
way of injunction, their respective, and if necessary exclusive rights
of occupation of the matrimonial home.   Hence the Matrimonial Homes
Act provides the criteria to be applied.   Further, in Lee v. Lee[14] it
was held that the same principles apply to cohabitants, that is, a
"man and a woman who are living with each other in the same household
as husband and wife",[15] even though the Matrimonial Homes Act itself
only extends to spouses.

The Matrimonial Homes Act criteria

3.8   Under section 1(3) of the Matrimonial Homes Act 1983, the
court may make such order as it thinks "just and reasonable having
regard to the conduct of the spouses in relation to each other and
otherwise, their respective needs and financial resources, to the
needs of any children and to all the circumstances of the case ....."
None of the statutory criteria is expressed to be paramount over any
other.   The majority of the House of Lords in Richards v. Richards

---

12. Bassett v. Bassett [1975] Fam. 76; Walker v. Walker [1978] 1
    W.L.R. 533; Samson v. Samson [1982] 1 W.L.R. 252; cf. Elsworth v.
    Elsworth (1979) 1 F.L.R. 245; Myers v. Myers [1982] 1 W.L.R. 247.

13. [1984] A.C. 174.

14. [1984] F.L.R. 243.

15. Domestic Violence and Matrimonial Proceedings Act 1976, s.1(2).

rejected the argument that the welfare of any children should be the first and paramount consideration.[16] In addition to these statutory criteria, the Court of Appeal has repeatedly emphasised the "draconian" nature of an ouster order.[17]

(a)   Conduct

3.9   The 1983 Act refers to the conduct of the spouses in relation to each other and otherwise. Although it has been said that in some cases other factors must prevail over the rights and wrongs between the adults,[18] the general effect of the decision in Richards has been to require proof of matrimonial misbehaviour on the part of the respondent which is worse than that of the applicant.[19] In Wiseman v. Simpson[20] the Court of Appeal rejected the contention that there must necessarily be violence or molestation, but there is considerable uncertainty about what sort of conduct will be thought sufficient.[21]

---

16. As is provided by Guardianship of Minors Act 1971, s.1 in any proceedings where the "legal custody or upbringing" of a minor is in issue. Lord Scarman held that this section did apply to ouster cases.

17. E.g. Summers v. Summers [1986] 1 F.L.R. 343; Wiseman v. Simpson [1988] 1 W.L.R. 35; Shipp v. Shipp [1988] 1 F.L.R. 347; Whitlock v. Whitlock [1989] 1 F.L.R. 208.

18. Lee v. Lee [1984] F.L.R. 243.

19. See e.g. Wiseman v. Simpson [1988] 1 W.L.R. 35 where Ralph Gibson L.J. emphasised that not only must the case of one party be stronger than that of the other but also such as to justify the making of an ouster order.

20. [1988] 1 W.L.R. 35.

21. There appears to be no reported case in the Court of Appeal since Richards of ouster in circumstances other than violence; before that time, there were several; e.g. Jones v. Jones [1971] 1 W.L.R. 396; Walker v. Walker [1978] 1 W.L.R. 533; Spindlow v. Spindlow [1979] Fam. 52.

3.10   To what extent, for example, is the test the same as that for a divorce on the basis that one party has behaved in such a way that the other cannot reasonably be expected to live with him?[22]   Given that this does not necessarily involve any judgment as to which was the more at fault, the test in ouster cases may be more stringent.[23] If so, does it amount to what would have been cruelty, or at least just cause for living apart, under the old law of the matrimonial offence?[24]   To what extent can such standards be applied to unmarried couples, who have never undertaken a legal obligation to live together?

3.11   The test suggested in _Richards_ itself was, in effect, the reasonableness of the applicant's wish to live apart from the respondent.[25]   That is by no means the same thing as a detailed examination of the marital rights and wrongs. However, other cases[26] have tended in that direction. It has also been emphasised that where issues of conduct are disputed, they cannot be tried on the basis of affidavit evidence alone.[27]   The court may therefore be obliged to hold a full-scale trial of the parties' relative matrimonial blameworthiness in order to resolve the short term question of how they should be accommodated pending their divorce.

---

22. Matrimonial Causes Act 1973, s.1(2)(b).

23. See e.g. O'Malley v. O'Malley [1982] 1 W.L.R. 244 where it appears that a divorce was granted but an ouster order refused.

24. This was superseded for divorce and judicial separation by the Divorce Reform Act 1969 and for matrimonial proceedings in magistrates' courts by the Domestic Proceedings and Magistrates' Courts Act 1978.

25. [1984] A.C. 174, 224 per Lord Brandon.

26. E.g. in Whitlock v. Whitlock [1989] 1 F.L.R. 208 where a full examination was required even though some violence had been admitted.

27. Harris v. Harris [1986] 1 F.L.R. 12; Shipp v. Shipp [1988] 1 F.L.R. 345; Whitlock v. Whitlock [1989] 1 F.L.R. 208.

(b)   The parties' respective needs and financial resources

3.12   As far as accommodation is concerned, if there is only one
matrimonial home,[28] it is obvious that the parent who retains actual
care and control of any child or children of the family will be the
more in need of housing.   In Wiseman v. Simpson,[29] however, it was
held that it was not "just or reasonable" to make such an order merely
because of the mother's greater need for accommodation.   The woman in
this case had excluded her male partner by changing the locks.   The
man, who was the father of her three month old son, applied under the
1976 Act for an order, inter alia, that she permit him to return to
the local authority flat of which they were joint tenants.   She
successfully cross-applied for an order excluding him from the flat.
The county court found that as there was no alternative accommodation
for the mother and child and as the applicant could live with his
parents an ouster order should be granted.   The applicant's appeal was
allowed and the draconian nature of ousting a person from his home
reiterated.[30]

3.13   The availability of alternative housing depends not only on
the parties' respective needs and financial situation but also on the

---

28. If the matrimonial home is large enough an application for an
ouster order may be refused on the basis that the parties could
live separately in the same house. See e.g. Anderson v. Anderson
[1984] F.L.R. 566. However in this case the registrar's refusal
was overruled. The wife shared a two bedroomed flat with her
husband, was at some risk of violence, and was 8 months pregnant.
The Court of Appeal found that the registrar had omitted to
consider the impact that would be made when a new baby was brought
into the home.

29. Wiseman v. Simpson [1988] 1 W.L.R. 35.

30. cf. Thurley v. Smith [1984] F.L.R. 875 where the court concluded
that the balance of respective needs of the parties lay in favour
of granting an ouster order to the wife who, unlike the husband,
might expect after some indefinable length of time to be rehoused
by the local authority. The wife was living in an overcrowded
refuge with her 8 year old son. The case may be distinguished
because the applicant in this case was subjected to violence.

available housing stock. The party who is most in need of the family home may also be the one who is most likely, because she is responsible for looking after the children, to have a priority claim to be rehoused as a homeless person. Frequently the courts are asked to take into account the claims of each party to be rehoused by the local authority.[31] It has been suggested that such expectations involve the courts in housing management decisions otherwise considered to be the peculiar province of public sector housing departments.[32] This inter-relationship between the law regulating domestic disputes and public housing allocation has become more pronounced since the enactment of the Housing Act 1980,[33] which provides that joint tenants both enjoy "secure" status, even when one of them is temporarily or permanently absent.[34] Hence the local authority no longer has the power to transfer tenancies between parties when a relationship breaks down.[35] At present, therefore, any deadlock can only be solved by matrimonial remedies which are not always available.[36]

---

[31]. In Thurley v. Smith [1984] 5 F.L.R. 875 it was held that one of the factors to be taken into account when considering the needs of the parties was the duty of the local authority to provide accommodation for homeless persons under the Housing (Homeless Persons) Act 1977, now consolidated in the Housing Act 1985. See also Wootton v Wootton [1984] F.L.R. 871.

[32]. See e.g., Ormrod L.J. in Warwick v. Warwick (1982) 3 F.L.R. 393.

[33]. Now consolidated in the Housing Act 1985.

[34]. A tenant will normally only lose his security by involuntary means either if successful proceedings for possession are brought by the local authority under one of the grounds laid down in Sch.2 of the Act or if the court makes an order transfering the tenancy under the Matrimonial Homes Act 1983, Sch.1, or the Matrimonial Causes Act 1973, s.24.

[35]. A co-tenant may unilaterally end a joint tenancy by serving notice to quit on the landlord; see London Borough of Greenwich v. McGrady (1983) 81 L.G.R. 288. However, there is no statutory obligation on the local authority to rehouse either party.

[36]. See D. Pearl, "Public Housing Allocation and Domestic Disputes",

(c)   The needs of any children

3.14   One of the effects of Richards is that a previous line of
authority, which gave priority to the interests of the children and
discouraged attempts to allocate blame where their welfare was at
stake, is overruled.[37]   A distinction was drawn, Lord Scarman
dissenting, between proceedings in which a child's custody,
upbringing, or property was a matter directly in issue and ouster
proceedings between parents, where those matters arose only
incidentally.[38]   However, it was emphasised in Lee v. Lee[39] that the
court has to take all the circumstances into account, decide what
weight is to be given to each, and balance one factor against another
in order to decide what is just and reasonable in the particular case.
In that case, it was decided that little weight should be given to the
parties' conduct but "by far the greater weight" should be given to
the needs of the children to re-establish the family unit in the
family home.

3.15   The alternative jurisdictions available to protect children
are considered in Part IV.[40]   Where ouster and wardship proceedings
are heard together, the Court of Appeal has held that the correct
procedure where care and control of the child is at issue, is first to

---

36. Continued
   in M.D.A. Freeman (ed), Essays in Family Law (1986);   M. Wright,
   "Ouster Orders and Housing Need" (1988) 19 N.L.J. 594;   C. Williams,
   "Ouster Orders, Property Adjustment and Council Housing" (1988) 19
   Fam.Law 438; R. Thornton, "Homelessness through Relationship
   Breakdown: The Local Authorities' Response" [1989] J.S.W.L. 67.

37. Phillips v. Phillips [1973] 1 W.L.R. 615;   Bassett v. Bassett
   [1975] Fam. 76;   Walker v. Walker [1978] 1 W.L.R. 533; Samson v.
   Samson [1982] 1 W.L.R. 252.

38. Richards v. Richards [1984] A.C. 174, 203.

39. [1984] F.L.R. 243, 248.

40. See paras. 4.14 et seq. below.

determine the care application according to the welfare principle and then take that decision into account as one, and only one, relevant consideration in the ouster decision according to section 1(3) of the Matrimonial Homes Act 1983.[41]

(d)   All the circumstances of the case

3.16   It is difficult to know what other factors may be thought relevant under this head. For example, excluding the husband to allow the dust to settle and to facilitate a reconciliation has been found not to be a relevant consideration.[42]   However, it has been stressed that every application must be dealt with on its own merits and that there may be cases in which the facts were such that one of the statutory criteria predominates in reaching a decision on what was "just and reasonable" in all the circumstances of the case.[43]   For this reason, those cases disapproved by Richards as erring in principle may nevertheless have been rightly decided on the facts.[44]

The Domestic Proceedings and Magistrates' Courts Act criteria

3.17   The criteria for granting exclusion orders under the Domestic Proceedings and Magistrates' Courts Act 1978 are: first, that the respondent has (a) used violence against the person of the applicant or a child of the family, or (b) threatened to use violence against the applicant or child and actually used it against someone else, or (c) threatened to use violence against applicant or child in breach of a personal protection order; and secondly, that applicant or child "is

---

[41.] Re T. (A Minor: Wardship); T. v. T. (Ouster Order) [1987] 1 F.L.R. 181.

[42.] Summers v. Summers [1986] 1 F.L.R. 343.

[43.] Ibid. 346.

[44.] See Richards v. Richards [1984] A.C. 174, 199 per Lord Hailsham.

in danger of being physically injured by the respondent".[45] The danger need not be imminent, but it must be objectively observable and not simply in the mind of the applicant alone.[46]

3.18   Although, clearly, the substantive effect of an exclusion order under the 1978 Act is the same as an ouster injunction or order under the Matrimonial Homes Act 1983, it does not appear to have been suggested that the magistrates should apply the Matrimonial Homes Act criteria in addition to those set out in the 1978 Act. Although limited to cases of violence, these appear to create an expectation that protection will be afforded.[47]

Criticisms of the present law

3.19   The reasoning of the House of Lords in _Richards_ v. _Richards_ has attracted serious criticism.[48]   More importantly, for our purposes, the position which has since developed could be thought unsatisfactory for a number of reasons.   First, the application of the Matrimonial Homes Act criteria to all cases fails to distinguish between the very different situations in which exclusion may be sought: (i) there may be an immediate need for protection against violence or other forms of abuse; (ii) there may be an immediate need to regulate a couple's short term accommodation needs in a period of disharmony, possibly leading up to divorce; (iii) where the couple

---

45. s.16(3).

46. _McCartney_ v. _McCartney_ [1981] 1 All E.R. 597.

47. Cf. _Myers_ v. _Myers_ [1982] 1 W.L.R. 247, a Domestic Violence Act case approved on the merits in _Richards_ v. _Richards_ [1984] A.C. 174, where there was violence which the court appeared to think excusable.

48. E.g. J. Eekelaar, "The Emergence of Children's Rights" (1986) 6 O.J.L.S. 161.

have mutual rights of occupation in the home, there may be a need for a longer term adjustment of those rights.

3.20   Secondly, the criteria were first enacted in 1967 before many of the most significant developments in this field: before the awakening of public concern in the problems of violence and abuse within the family;[49] before the replacement of the doctrine of the matrimonial offence with the concept of irretrievable breakdown of the marriage as the sole ground for divorce;[50] before the introduction of powers of property adjustment on divorce;[51] and before any serious consideration had been given to the problems of cohabiting couples and their children.   As the 1967 Act was principally designed to give protection against dispositions to third parties, the original purpose was to identify those non-owning spouses who were sufficiently deserving of long term accommodation in the family home to entitle them to resist such dispositions.

3.21   Hence the criteria could be said to give inadequate protection against violence, by requiring conduct to be balanced against other factors, and not acknowledging that in such cases personal protection for the victims should be given priority over the hardship to respondent.[52]   Although the remedy is discretionary in magistrates' courts, there is no indication in the 1978 Act that the court should be investigating any mitigating factors in the violence or that it must be serious if it is to justify the victim in her

---

49. Stimulated principally by Erin Pizzey, Scream Quietly or the Neighbours will Hear (1974), followed by the Report of the Committee on Violence in Marriage, HC 553 (1974-75).

50. Divorce Reform Act 1969, in force 1 January 1971.

51. Matrimonial Proceedings and Property Act 1970, in force 1 January 1971.

52. S. Parker, "The Legal Background", in J. Pahl (ed), Private Violence and Public Policy (1985), argues that the effect is that the court must consider whether the respondent's conduct warrants the likely consequences to him of being excluded, rather than focusing upon its effect upon the victims.

desire to live apart for a while. The success rate for applications for injunctions under the 1976 Act is high, but there is considerable variation over the country. Magistrates, on the other hand, refuse very few applications.[53]

3.22   A further criticism, relating to cases in which an ouster injunction is sought during marital breakdown and where divorce proceedings have already begun or are being considered by one or both parties, is of the necessity for holding a trial of the parties' conduct at this interlocutory stage. Allegations of violence or of other types of unacceptable behaviour constituting conduct relevant to the granting of ouster injunctions may also be cited in an existing or subsequent divorce petition based on the respondent's "behaviour" under section 1(2)(d) of the Matrimonial Causes Act 1973.[54] The court is then placed in the difficult position of having to make findings of fact for one purpose in advance of the trial of the same issue for another purpose.[55] A further result of pre-divorce litigation involving issues of conduct is that it is likely, on the one hand, to cause delay in just those cases where a leaving should take place quickly, and on the other hand, to impede reconciliation, where that is appropriate, by protracted battles between the parties as to

---

[53.] L. Smith, <u>Domestic Violence: an overview of the literature</u> (1989), pp.90-91; M. Murch et al, <u>The Overlapping Family Jurisdictions of Magistrates' Courts and County Courts</u> (1987), found that solicitors frequently favour magistrates' courts for personal protection orders when speed is the important factor.

[54.] See, e.g., <u>Baynham</u> v. <u>Baynham</u>, [1968] 1 W.L.R. 1890, the first case to come before the court under the Matrimonial Homes Act 1967, where the Court of Appeal made an interim exclusion order, even though the full investigation into the conduct of the spouses required by s.1(3) of the Act had not been made because such questions in issue between the parties would be decided in the divorce proceedings which were at that time pending. This case would now be disapproved under <u>Richards</u> v. <u>Richards</u> principles.

[55.] Cf., e.g., <u>Parris</u> v. <u>Parris</u> (1974) Fam. Law 77, where Stamp L.J. deplored the use of such hearings to engage in pre-trial battles on allegations of behaviour arising in the divorce suit.

allegations of not only past, but continuing conduct. This is contrary to the general trend of divorce law in reducing the need for recrimination and fault-finding, with all the bitterness and conflict which this can entail. It is a particular cause for concern that the need to provide a period of calm during which the parties may perhaps become reconciled has been held to be irrelevant.[56]

3.23   Above all, criticism has been made of the risk that the children's welfare will be given insufficient weight in the balancing exercise.[57] In _Richards_ itself, there was no evidence at all that the children's welfare was suffering from the presence of both parties in the home: quite the reverse, as the couple had made arrangements to share their care between them. In _Summers_ v. _Summers_,[58] however, the judge found that it was not in the children's interests to witness continuing bitter quarrels between the parties in which (it appears) furniture was broken and objects smashed. He also thought that it would be beneficial for all to have a break for some time. It was held that he appeared to have given too much weight to the interests of the children as against the draconian nature of the order, where the couple were equally to blame for the situation which had developed. This is inconsistent with the general trend of the law to give increased, if not predominating weight to the interests of children, even in relation to matters of finance and property. Thus the Matrimonial and Family Proceedings Act 1984 requires courts, when dealing with financial provision and property adjustment after divorce, to give "first consideration" to the welfare of any children of the family who are under eighteen.[59]

---

56. _Summers_ v. _Summers_ [1986] 1 F.L.R. 343.

57. E.g. J. Eekelaar, _op. cit._ (1986); S. Edwards and A. Halpern, "Conflicting Interests: Protecting Children or Protecting Title to Property" [1988] J.S.W.L. 110.

58. [1986] 1 F.L.R. 343.

59. Matrimonial Causes Act 1973, s.25(1) as substituted by the Matrimonial and Family Proceedings Act 1984, s.3.

3.24   The courts have often referred to the draconian nature of an
ouster order, and indeed its effects will often be severe,
particularly if it is granted at short notice without giving much time
to arrange alternative accommodation.   This in itself can produce
circular arguments, where the remedy is thought so severe that it is
only appropriate where the risk of harm is such that it must be
granted in terms which increase its severity.[60]   Yet there are
obviously cases in which one of the parties can arrange alternative
accommodation, with family or friends or commercially, at least for a
short time and without suffering severe or even appreciable hardship.
There are equally obviously cases where the hardship caused to one
party if the other is allowed to remain will be much more severe than
the effects of ouster.   Thus although it will often be a severe
remedy, the assumption that it is so in all cases can obscure the
considerable differences between the circumstances of the parties and
in which the remedy is sought.   Even where it is severe, it may be the
only proper solution to the problem.

3.25   Finally, the 1967 criteria are not easily applicable to cases
between unmarried couples.   There is, for example, no indication of
the relevance, if any, of their respective property rights.   As
between married couples, the Matrimonial Homes Act 1983 provides
mutual rights of occupation and procedures specifically designed to
enforce or adjust these irrespective of whether the couple intend to
divorce.   On divorce or judicial separation, the Matrimonial Causes
Act 1973 gives power to adjust the property rights themselves.[61]
Neither statute applies to unmarried couples, who will normally have

---

60. See, e.g., Burke v. Burke [1987] 2 F.L.R. 71, where the Court of
    Appeal held that although the judge at first instance had found
    that it was just and reasonable to make an ouster order, he had
    exercised his discretion wrongly in suspending the effect of the
    order for 8 weeks.   A period of 2 weeks was substituted.

61. s.24.

to resort to actions under the ordinary law unless they can obtain relief under section 1 of the 1976 Act.[62]

Anti-molestation and personal protection orders

3.26   The Domestic Violence and Matrimonial Proceedings Act 1976 gives county courts power to grant injunctions against molestation of the applicant or any child living with the applicant even though no other proceedings are pending before the court.[63] Similar injunctions may be granted in divorce or other matrimonial proceedings.

3.27   The precise scope of the order may be tailored to the needs of the individual case, but a common form will restrain the respondent from "assaulting, molesting, annoying or otherwise interfering with the applicant or any child living with the applicant". Before an injunction can be granted there has to be some evidence of molestation.[64] Molestation includes, but is wider than, violence.

> "Violence is a form of molestation but molestation may take place without the threat or use of violence and still be serious and inimical to mental and physical health."[65]

"Pester" has been suggested as a synonym,[66] and it has also been said that molestation applies to any conduct which can properly be regarded

---

62. For deficiencies of ordinary law in this respect, see paras. 4.9-4.10 below.

63. s.1(1)(a) and (b).

64. Spindlow v. Spindlow [1979] Fam. 52.

65. Davis v. Johnson [1979] A.C. 264, 334 per Viscount Dilhorne.

66. Vaughan v. Vaughan [1973] 1 W.L.R. 1159, 1162. A husband was held to have molested his wife when he called at her place of work, and made a "perfect nuisance of himself the whole time".

as such a degree of harassment as to call for the intervention of the court.[67] Hence the relief available under the 1976 Act or in matrimonial causes covers a wide range of behaviour which can cause particular problems when a family relationship is breaking down but which does not necessarily involve the commission of a tort. However, it has recently been held that there is no tort of harassment in English law, and hence no protection for those who do not fall within the ambit of the Act.[68]

3.28   Experience in the family jurisdiction clearly indicates that such protection is needed between spouses and cohabitants. However, the lack of a clear statutory definition of molestation could be criticised. In general molestation may be described either by the form that the objectionable conduct takes or by the effect that it has on the applicant who suffers from it. On the one hand, it is only fair that the enjoined person knows exactly what types of behaviour would constitute a breach of the court's order and formal definition would also promote consistency between courts; on the other hand, it might be argued that as the form and effect of molestation varies so much according to circumstance any sufficiently embracing definition would be hard to formulate. The respondent's past behaviour and present motive may also be relevant. For example, sitting in a parked car outside someone's home or workplace is not objectionable in itself, unless and until it is perceived as part of a pattern of conduct with no purpose other than that of unsettling or intimidating the person concerned.

---

[67]. Horner v. Horner [1982] Fam. 90; after the wife had obtained a personal protection order in the magistrates' court the husband stopped using violence or threatening violence against her, but harassed her in other ways, such as handing her menacing letters, intercepting her on the way to work; it was held that she should be granted an injunction against molestation under the 1976 Act.

[68]. See e.g. Patel v. Patel [1988] 2 F.L.R. 197, para. 4.12 below.

3.29   Under section 16(2) of the Domestic Proceedings and Magistrates' Courts Act 1978, the court may grant an order that the respondent shall not use or threaten to use violence against the applicant or a child of the family.[69] The court must be satisfied on the balance of probabilities that violence or the threat of it has taken place and also that the order is "necessary" for the protection of the applicant or child.[70]

3.30   Violence is not defined in the 1978 Act, and this again could be criticised.   The concept of violence does not generally include mental injury, actual or threatened, or harassment. The use of force is technically an assault and therefore violent, although if of a minor nature, e.g. pushing, might not be considered of the degree necessary to satisfy the court that violence has taken place.   The violence must be directed against the applicant or child and violence against property or the person of others is not included.

3.31   Personal protection remedies available in magistrates' courts are therefore less extensive than those available in the higher courts under the Domestic Violence and Matrimonial Proceedings Act 1976 or matrimonial proceedings. If an applicant is being harassed, pestered or molested in a non-violent way, for example, by following or telephoning, then no remedy is available under the 1978 Act and an application under the 1976 Act will have to be made in the county court.[71] The number of applications made to the magistrates' courts has been steadily falling since 1984 and the wider and more extensive

---

69. By s.16(10), the court may include a provision that the respondent shall not invite or assist any other person to use or threaten to use violence against applicant or child.

70. s.16(2).

71. As in <u>Horner</u> v. <u>Horner</u> [1982] Fam. 90, 92, where Ormrod L.J. observed that "It is perhaps a pity that there should be two courts sitting in the same area dealing with very similar problems, but with significantly different powers."

range of remedies and powers available in the county courts is likely to be a contributory factor.[72] Molestation was originally excluded because it was thought to turn on psychological harm and magistrates were not equipped to adjudicate in matters requiring expert evidence.[73] In practice, however, expert evidence is rarely required in county courts in such cases.

Short or long term remedies?

3.32   Under the Matrimonial Homes Act 1983, an order may be made to have effect for a specified period or until further order.[74] Similarly, the practice in pending matrimonial causes was to grant relief until decree or some other point in the proceedings. However, in Davis v. Johnson[75] it was emphasised that an ouster injunction in proceedings under the Domestic Violence and Matrimonial Proceedings Act 1976 was essentially a temporary or short-term remedy. This was confirmed in a Practice Note which stated that:

> "It is within the discretion of the court to decide whether an injunction should be granted and, if so, for how long it should operate. But whenever an injunction is granted excluding one of the parties from the matrimonial home (or a part thereof or specified area), consideration should be given to imposing a

---

72.   In 1987 (Home Office Statistical Bulletin, 20/1988) about 6,000 applications were made under the Domestic Proceedings and Magistrates' Courts Act 1978 continuing the decline from the peak of 8,700 in 1984. The numbers of applications made under the Domestic Violence and Matrimonial Proceedings Act 1976 has increased throughout that period. See also M. Murch, The Overlapping Family Jurisdiction of Magistrates' Courts and County Courts (1987), which highlights regional variations.

73.   (1976) Law Com.No.77, para.3.12.

74.   s.1(4).

75.   Davis v. Johnson [1979] A.C. 264, 343 per Lord Salmon, the Act provides "first aid but not intensive care"; also Ormrod L.J. in Hopper v. Hopper [1978] 1 W.L.R. 1342, 1344.

time limit on the operation of the injunction. In most cases a period of up to three months is likely to suffice, at least in the first instance. It will be open to the respondent in any event to apply for the discharge of the injunction before the expiry of the period fixed, for instance on the ground of reconciliation, and to the applicant to apply for an extension."[76]

The Practice Note does not fetter the judge's discretion and in appropriate cases, for example, where there has been persistent disregard of previous orders of the court, the court may grant an ouster injunction "until further order".[77] However, it appears to cover all types of ouster injunction, whether under the 1976 Act or in matrimonial proceedings. It is not clear whether the courts are also to follow these general guidelines in ordinary proceedings under the Matrimonial Homes Act 1983.

3.33   The Domestic Proceedings and Magistrates' Courts Act 1978 provides that personal protection orders may be issued for such term and subject to such exceptions or conditions as may be specified.[78] No specific time limits have been laid down in relation to the duration of exclusion orders made by the magistrates' courts.

3.34   The three-month guideline may be appropriate in some cases but causes difficulty in some of the procedures with which we are concerned. As between unmarried couples, the 1976 Act introduced new

---

76. Practice Direction (Injunctions: Domestic Violence) [1978] 1 W.L.R. 1123

77. E.g. Spencer v. Camacho [1983] 4 F.L.R. 662; Galan v. Galan [1985] F.L.R 905, where injunctions were granted "until further order".

78. s.16(9).

remedies over and above those available under the general law.[79] Where the applicant has no right to occupy the premises, it is understandable that these were regarded as short term "first aid" relief until the applicant could find alternative accommodation.[80] Nevertheless, a recent Home Office study observes that "the practice of restricting injunctions to a three month time limit has also been shown by research to aggravate victims' problems by not allowing sufficient time to make suitable arrangements, especially with regard to accommodation".[81]

3.35   Where, as may be increasingly common, an unmarried couple are both entitled to occupy the premises, the difficulty is that there is no procedure or jurisdiction comparable to that in the Matrimonial Homes Act for regulating their respective rights. If they are joint owners, an application for sale under section 30 of the Law of Property Act 1925 may take some time.[82] Furthermore, there is no simple procedure for determining claims to a beneficial interest in property to which only one is legally entitled, comparable to that under section 17 of the Married Women's Property Act 1882 for married or engaged couples.[83] If they are joint tenants of rented property, there is no means of resolving disputes between them and if the tenancy is secure, the landlord has no power to transfer it.[84]   In

---

79. Davis v. Johnson [1979] A.C. 264; see para. 2.12 above.

80. See e.g. Freeman v. Collins (1983) 4 F.L.R. 649, where an order without limit of time was limited on appeal to one month, as the woman had no legal or equitable interest in the property.

81. L. Smith, Domestic Violence: an overview of the literature, Home Office Research Study No.107 (1989), p.90.

82. The £30,000 limit on the jurisdiction of county courts in property matters means that most such cases must begin in the High Court except by agreement; County Courts Act 1984, s.24.

83. The summary county court procedure under the 1882 Act can be used within three years of the ending of an engagement to marry; Law Reform (Miscellaneous Provisions) Act 1970, s.2(2).

84. Para. 3.13 above.

these circumstances it is not surprising that the courts have on occasions used the 1976 Act in order to resolve matters.[85]

3.36   As between married couples, there are now remedies for resolving disputes about occupation irrespective of whether or not they are joint tenants or owners,[86] which were clearly intended to be available longer term or indefinitely if need be. Given the existence of such a long term remedy, and the thoroughness of the examination which now has to take place before an injunction can be granted, it would often be an unnecessary and costly duplication of effort if proceedings begun under the 1976 Act were generally to result in short-term but renewable orders. It appears that this is not the view taken in magistrates' courts, where an exclusion order can have the practical effect of an indefinite order under the Matrimonial Homes Act. In proceedings for divorce, nullity or judicial separation the court also has power to transfer or adjust the parties' rights in the property itself.[87] It may be often be convenient, therefore, to grant relief until an appropriate point in those proceedings, whether it be the decree or the resolution of a claim for property adjustment.

3.37   The Practice Note, of course, is not intended to lay down an inflexible "three-month rule". Nevertheless, there may be a case for more comprehensive and flexible guidelines, which distinguish the circumstances in which time-limited and indefinite orders are appropriate.

---

85. E.g. Spindlow v. Spindlow [1979] Fam. 52; Spencer v. Camacho [1983] 4 F.L.R. 662.

86. Matrimonial Homes Act 1983, ss.1 and 9.

87. Under the Matrimonial Causes Act 1973, s.24; or if the property is held under a protected, statutory, secure or assured tenancy, under the Matrimonial Homes Act 1983, s.7 and Sched.1.

PART IV

THE PEOPLE PROTECTED

4.1   In this Part we consider the range of people who are protected under the existing law. All the remedies discussed in Part III are available on the application of husbands or wives, but problems arise in relation to former spouses. Some protection is provided for cohabitants and for children, but it may also be necessary to look to other remedies available to them. Other family members are not covered at all and must look to the general law for their protection.

Divorced spouses

4.2   Most of the remedies discussed in Part III are no longer available once the spouses are divorced. A former spouse cannot apply to a magistrates' court under the 1978 Act; nor can she apply under section 1 of the Domestic Violence and Matrimonial Proceedings Act 1976, unless the couple are still "living with each other in the same household as husband and wife" after the decree.[1] Further, where only one spouse is legally entitled to occupy the home, the rights of occupation enjoyed by the other under the Matrimonial Homes Act come to an end on divorce, unless "in the event of a matrimonial dispute or estrangement" the court has directed otherwise during the marriage.[2] The power to restrict or suspend the occupation rights of an owning spouse ends at divorce.[3]

---

1. 1976 Act, s.1(2).

2. 1983 Act, ss.1(10) and 2(4).

3. See M. v. M. (Custody Application) [1988] 1 F.L.R. 225, 235 per Booth J.

4.3   It might be thought that these limitations cause few problems. By definition, there will be divorce proceedings in which an anti-molestation order may be granted.   It has long been accepted that an injunction granted before decree absolute may be continued thereafter, or even granted for the first time after the decree.[4] This may be justified in support of a general right not to be assaulted or molested.[5]   The courts appear ready to assume that spouses and former spouses have a right to be protected against molestation even though there is no general right to be protected against harassment.[6]   Regrettably, such protection is sometimes very necessary against former spouses who find it impossible to accept that the relationship is over.

4.4   As for exclusion or ouster, although rights of occupation come to an end, the divorce court has power to adjust the parties' respective rights to the property itself,[7] including a power to order the transfer of a protected, statutory, secure or assured tenancy.[8] However, there is frequently some lapse of time between decree absolute and the conclusion of these ancillary matters.   During this time, the former spouses may continue to share the matrimonial home and this can be a source of considerable strain for both the parties and any children.   The earlier authorities,[9] which recognised a power

---

4. Robinson v. Robinson [1965] P.39; Montgomery v. Montgomery [1965] P.46;

5. E.g. Wilde v. Wilde [1988] 2 F.L.R. 83, 92 per Bingham L.J.

6. See further paras. 4.12 - 4.13 below.

7. Matrimonial Causes Act 1973, s.24.

8. Matrimonial Homes Act 1983, s.7 and Sched.1.

9. E.g. Stewart v. Stewart [1973] Fam.21; Adams v. Adams (1965) 109 S.J. 899; Phillips v. Phillips [1973] 1 W.L.R. 615; cf. O'Malley v. O'Malley [1982] 1 W.L.R. 244; Brent v. Brent [1975] Fam.1; Waugh v. Waugh (1982) 3 F.L.R. 375.   All these cases turned on whether or not there were children living in the home whose interests required protection.

to exclude one party in some circumstances, have now to be considered in the light of the decision in Richards v. Richards,[10] which emphasised that ouster injunctions could only be granted in accordance with the Matrimonial Homes Act or in support of some other right recognised in law.

4.5   A former spouse with no proprietory interest in the home probably has no right which could found an exclusion order even if a claim for the transfer of the home is pending.[11] Even when they are joint owners or tenants, prima facie each is entitled to occupy and neither can exclude the other.[12] The only basis for doing so would be that one had by his violence or other behaviour made it impossible for the other to exercise her own rights while he was there.[13] None of the recent cases between divorced spouses involved violence or conduct of such a nature. There are also conflicting decisions in the Court of Appeal as to whether an inherent jurisdiction to exclude one parent from the home in the interests of the children of the family, which was recognised in the earlier cases, can be reconciled with Richards v. Richards.[14]

4.6   Hence while there exists power to protect against violence and molestation after divorce, which in cases where this makes it impossible for one former spouse to exercise her own right to occupy the home may include a power to exclude the other, there is no general

---

10. [1984] A.C. 174.

11. O'Malley v. O'Malley [1982] 1 W.L.R. 244; M. v. M. (Custody Application) [1988] 1 F.L.R. 225, 236 per Booth J.

12. See e.g. Waugh v. Waugh (1982) 3 F.L.R. 375, 379 per Ormrod L.J.; Ainsbury v. Millington [1986] 1 All.E.R. 73, 76 per Dillon L.J.

13. See Davis v. Johnson [1979] A.C. 264, 330 per Lord Diplock; also Gurasz v. Gurasz [1970] P.11.

14. Wilde v. Wilde [1988] 2 F.L.R. 83; M. v. M. (Custody Application) [1988] 1 F.L.R. 225.

power to adjust the parties' respective rights of occupation. Further, because they are no longer man and wife, the court cannot attach a power of arrest under section 2 of the Domestic Violence and Matrimonial Homes Act 1976 to injunctions against violence.[15]

Cohabitants

4.7   The Domestic Violence and Matrimonial Proceedings Act 1976 was entirely novel in that it extended personal protection remedies available to a husband and wife to those living together in the same household as husband and wife.[16]   It was intended to apply to those living together "on a stable basis"[17]   The question whether a couple are living together as husband and wife is one of fact.   In Adeoso v. Adeoso[18] the Court of Appeal held that the words of the statute were not to be interpreted literally and were intended to describe the nature of a couple's relationship not their living arrangements at the time of application.   Further, what on an "objective view" looked like a marriage-type relationship, even one of the last stages of break-up, constituted living together as husband and wife.   The question of how long after the relationship has come to an end the jurisdiction of the 1976 Act will be exercised is one to which a number of approaches have been canvassed.[19]   The problem has been clearly stated by Cumming-Bruce L.J:

[15.] Harrison and Another v. Lewis; R. v. S. [1988] 2 F.L.R. 339.

[16.] s.1(2).

[17.] Official Report (H.C.), Standing Committee F, 30 June 1976, col.5, Jo Richardson M.P.

[18.] [1980] 1 W.L.R. 1535.

[19.] E.g. Mclean v. Nugent (1980) 1 F.L.R. 26; B. v. B. (Domestic Violence: Jurisdiction) [1978] Fam.26; O'Neill v. Williams [1984] F.L.R. 1.

"a literal interpretation does not give effect to the wishes of Parliament, for such a construction would have the effect that the very persons for whom the Act was designed to provide an urgent and practical remedy would, in the nature of things, usually be unable to invoke the jurisdiction."[20]

The courts have usually adopted a pragmatic approach, the general principle being that a remedy will continue to be available if it can be shown that the couple were living together until the events which led to the application being made. However, the longer the time that elapses between those events and the application, the harder it will be for the aggrieved partner to bring herself within the Act.[21]

4.8   Novel though the 1976 Act was, there are two serious limitations in the protection which it affords to cohabitants. First, there is no power to protect against violence or other molestation after the relationship has ended. Yet this may be just as necessary between people who were formerly living together as it is between divorced spouses. The alternative of proceeding in tort is not only more cumbersome, but may also run into difficulties as to the precise scope of the protection available against molestation. For example, a former cohabitant who has gone to live with her parents may not be entitled to seek an injunction to keep her partner away from her new home or from pestering her at her place of work.[22]

4.9   Secondly, as we have already seen,[23] there is no simple machinery for adjusting the parties' respective rights of occupation

---

20. White v. White [1983] Fam. 54, 63; O'Neill v. Williams [1984] F.L.R. 1.

21. E.g. Mclean v. Nugent (1979) 1 F.L.R. 26.

22. See para. 4.12 below.

23. Para. 3.35 above.

44

even where they are joint owners or tenants of the home. A striking illustration of this is Ainsbury v. Millington.[24] An unmarried couple with a baby were granted a joint tenancy of a council house. The respondent was then arrested and imprisoned for burglary. While he was in custody, their relationship ended and the applicant married another man. On release, the respondent returned to the home, whereupon (not surprisingly) the applicant left, with her husband and child. They went to stay with her mother, where conditions were overcrowded and unsatisfactory. The county court judge granted the applicant interim custody of the child but held that he had no jurisdiction to oust the respondent from the home so that they could return. The Court of Appeal, with evident reluctance, agreed. Dillon L.J. observed:

> "I find this case difficult and I do not find it satisfactory that there should be various statutory codes covering applications for ouster orders and somewhat of a limbo position where the statutory codes, for one reason or another, are not applicable."[25]

Ironically, while a couple who own their home may at least apply for a sale under section 30 of the Law of Property Act 1925, if it is rented there is nothing which either of them can do. Further, if it is rented under a protected, statutory, secure or assured tenancy, there is nothing which the landlord can do unless one is prepared to surrender the tenancy.[26]

4.10   A related difficulty is that disputes about occupation may be inextricably linked with disputes about ownership. Disputes between married couples can usually be resolved in a county court under

---

24. [1986] 1 All E.R. 73.

25. Ibid., p.77.

26. See para. 3.13 above.

section 17 of the Married Women's Property Act 1882,[27] as can disputes between engaged couples, provided that proceedings are brought within three years of the ending of the engagement.[28] Otherwise, the dispute may have to be resolved in the Chancery Division of the High Court. This can cause hardship, on the one hand, where a partner with a beneficial interest has been wrongly excluded from the home, or on the other hand, where a partner with the sole legal and beneficial interest finds it impossible to exclude the other pending the resolution of the High Court proceedings.

4.11   Unmarried partners cannot apply for personal protection or exclusion orders under the Domestic Proceedings and Magistrates' Court Act 1978. It might now be questioned whether it is proper to deny them these remedies. The jurisdiction of magistrates' courts is specifically designed to afford summary, local and inexpensive relief. This was a significant factor in giving them the power to grant both personal protection and exclusion orders in favour of spouses.[29] However, the number of applications made to magistrates' courts is falling, while the number of applications to county courts under the Domestic Violence and Matrimonial Proceedings Act 1976 is steadily increasing. In 1987 almost 70 per cent of those applications were for injunctions against molestation.[30] The statistics do not provide a breakdown by the marital status of the applicant, but it seems likely that pressure on the county courts could be considerably relieved by allowing cohabitants to apply to a magistrates' court. This would, however, require magistrates to resolve the sometimes difficult

---

[27]. There is now little need to resolve questions of legal or beneficial title between spouses, as divorce courts have wide powers to adjust these, under section 24 of the Matrimonial Causes Act 1973.

[28]. Law Reform (Miscellaneous Provisions) Act 1970, s.2(2).

[29]. (1976), Law Com. No.77, para. 3.15.

[30]. Home Office Statistical Bulletin, 20/1988; Judicial Statistics 1987, Table 5.17.

question of whether the parties were living together as husband and wife. Further, unless their powers were more limited than those between spouses, they might be called upon to decide questions of entitlement to occupy the home, which are particularly difficult in cases where the applicant claims a beneficial interest in a home of which the other is sole legal owner.

Other family members

4.12   The highly charged emotions which exist within families can sometimes lead to behaviour very similar to that against which spouses or cohabitants are given protection. In <u>Patel</u> v. <u>Patel</u>,[31] for example, the plaintiff's son-in-law had been "prosecuting a feud" against his father-in-law by trespassing on his home, threatening him in a number of ways, and abusing him in the street or at work. In an action for tort, an injunction was granted in the usual matrimonial terms, restraining the defendant from "assaulting, molesting or otherwise interfering" with the plaintiff, and from trespassing upon his property or approaching within 50 yards of it. This was later restricted to restraining him from assaulting or molesting the plaintiff or trespassing on his property. The Court of Appeal endorsed this restriction, on the grounds that the tort of trespass is not committed by coming within 50 yards of the home, nor is there a general tort of harassment.

4.13   The court upheld the injunction against molestation but without considering whether there is any distinction between harassment and molestation in the wide sense in which the latter is used in matrimonial cases.[32] Following this decision, it might now be questioned whether there is any general right not to be molested,

---

31. [1988] 2 F.L.R. 179.

32. See para. 3.27 above.

47

apart from the court's inherent power to protect litigants in pending proceedings from conduct which may prejudice their right to litigate and the express powers which are given by section 1(1)(a) and (b) of the 1976 Act.[33] There is little doubt that such remedies are needed between spouses and it could also be argued that there are special features about family relationships which would justify extending remedies against molestation, including harassment, to other family members.

Children

4.14   Injunctions can be granted under the Domestic Violence and Matrimonial Proceedings Act 1976 to protect the applicant and any child "living with" the applicant. Jo Richardson, the Member of Parliament who introduced the Bill, stated that it was undesirable to limit protection to particular children because the remedy was being provided in:

> "a factual situation of domestic upheaval, and the relationship of the child to the two parties is not really important".[34]

The child cannot apply on his own behalf for an order. Further, if one or more children are living with the respondent, and the applicant fears for their safety, an injunction cannot be granted under the 1976 Act to provide for their protection.

4.15   An ouster injunction may be sought under the Domestic Violence and Matrimonial Proceedings Act 1976 for the principal purpose of protecting a child living with the applicant from abuse, but the needs of that child will not be the paramount consideration. As clearly

---

[33]. See para. 2.11 above; see also Judge N. Fricker Q.C. "Molestation and harassment after _Patel_ v. _Patel_" (1988) 18 Fam. Law 395.

[34]. Official Report (H.C.), Standing Committee F, 30 June 1976, col.6.

stated in <u>Richards</u> v. <u>Richards</u>,[35] the principle enunciated in the Guardianship of Minors Act 1971 that the welfare of children is to be the first and paramount consideration, applies only to those proceedings in which the child's custody, upbringing, or property is the matter directly in issue. This will not be the case in ouster proceedings between parents, where strictly such matters arise only incidentally. Nor does the 1976 Act give any power to grant ouster orders between parents who have never been married or lived together as husband and wife.[36]

4.16   The jurisdiction of magistrates' courts to grant orders for the protection of children of married couples only extends to those minors who are "children of the family". The test is the same as it is in relation to financial provision:

> "a child of both parties; and any other child, not being a child who is being boarded-out with those parties by a local authority or voluntary organisation, who has been treated by both of those parties as a child of their family".[37]

A step-child must therefore be treated as a child of the family by both spouses for the provisions of the Domestic Proceedings and Magistrates' Court Act to apply. Foster children and any other children living with the family who do not fit the definition are excluded.

4.17   The question of non-molestation or ouster orders may also arise in custody proceedings under the Guardianship of Minors Act 1971 or in wardship. The High Court and county courts may grant

---

35. [1984] A.C. 174, 203. Lord Scarman dissenting.

36. See <u>Tuck</u> v. <u>Nicholls</u> [1989] 1 F.L.R. 283, para. 6.12 below.

37. Domestic Proceedings and Magistrates' Court Act 1978, s.88(1).

non-molestation injunctions for the protection of the child and the adult with custody or care and control.[38] It may also be possible to exclude a person from the home if he has no right to occupy it.[39] We have already seen that the authorities on whether a person with a right of occupation can be ousted for the sake of the children are inconsistent.[40] It seems clear that this cannot be done in proceedings under the Guardianship of Minors Act,[41] but there may be some doubt about whether it can be done in wardship.[42] As between married couples, of course, one spouse can always make an application under the Matrimonial Homes Act at the same time.[43] It remains to be seen whether the High Court would be prepared to use its wide powers in wardship to plug the gap so strikingly illustrated by Ainsbury v. Millington.[44] Wardship proceedings may be initiated by anyone, including local authorities. They might therefore be used to oust a person guilty or suspected of child abuse so that the child does not have to be removed from home. There is no statutory power to do this.

---

38. Re W. (A Minor) [1981] 3 All E.R. 401; Re H. (A Minor)(Injunction: Breach) [1986] 1 F.L.R. 558.

39. Re W. (A Minor) [1981] 3 All E.R. 401.

40. Para. 4.5 above.

41. Ainsbury v. Millington [1986] 1 All E.R. 73; M. v. M. (Custody Application) [1988] 1 F.L.R. 225.

42. Re V. (A Minor)(Wardship) (1979) 123 S.J. 201; Wilde v. Wilde [1988] 2 F.L.R. 83, although a divorce case, was based on the continued existence of an inherent power to protect children in this way.

43. See Re T. (A Minor) [1987] 1 F.L.R. 181, where a father made a Matrimonial Homes Act application in the course of wardship proceedings.

44. [1986] 1 All.E.R. 73; para. 4.9 above.

Applications by third parties

4.18   Where children are at risk of neglect or abuse, the responsibility for investigating and if necessary bringing proceedings to protect them from harm lies with local social services authorities.[45]   In the short term, place of safety orders may be obtained and in the longer term, applications for care or supervision orders can be made under the Children and Young Persons Act 1969 or in wardship.[46]   In the wake of the Report of the Inquiry into Child Abuse in Cleveland,[47] it has been suggested that it would in some cases be more appropriate to remove the abuser, or suspected abuser, from the home than to subject the child to all the upheaval and stigma involved.[48]   Under the Children Bill, now before Parliament, local authorities will no longer be able to seek care or supervision orders through the wardship jurisdiction, but they will be able to invoke it for other purposes which are not covered by the statutory scheme if there is a risk that the child will suffer harm.[49]   It is possible, therefore, that they will continue to seek to use wardship in order to oust the abuser or suspected abuser from the home.

4.19   One reform which might therefore be considered is to provide a statutory scheme for ouster in child protection cases. The question then arises of whether this would be better provided for by giving the

---

[45.] Children and Young Persons Act 1969, s.2(1),(2); see now Children Bill, clause 39.

[46.] Children and Young Persons Act 1969, ss.28(1) and 1(1) respectively; see now Children Bill [as amended in Standing Committee B], clauses 38 and 28; Family Law Reform Act 1969, s.7; cf. Children Bill, clause 84.

[47.] (1988) Cm. 412.

[48.] Official Report (H.C.), Standing Committee B, 25 May 1989, cols. 325-329. See Appendix A below.

[49.] Clause 84.

courts additional or alternative powers when hearing applications for emergency protection, care or supervision orders, or by giving local authorities power to apply on behalf of the child for remedies under the private law, or by some combination of the two.[50]

4.20   A further question is whether others should be able to initiate these remedies in order to lighten the burden of responsibility upon the adult victims involved.   In New South Wales, South Australia and Western Australia, domestic violence legislation provides for the police to make an application for a protection order on behalf of the "aggrieved spouse", where the assailant and the victim are married to each other, or living together in a "de facto" relationship.[51]   It is thought that the police bringing proceedings brings home to the respondent the seriousness of the matter.   In South Australia approximately 97% of orders are applied for by the police.[52] Standing to make a complaint in proceedings brought under recent family violence legislation in Victoria also extends to any person with the written consent of the person being victimised.[53]

[50.] See further Appendix A.

[51.] The Crimes (Domestic Violence) Amendment Act 1982 (NSW);   Peace and Good Behaviour Act 1982 (Qld);   Justices Amendment Act (No.2) 1982 (SA);   Justices Amendment Act 1982 (WA).

[52.] Domestic Violence (1986), The Law Reform Commission (Australia), Report No.30, para.92, n.7.

[53.] The Crimes (Family Violence) Act 1987, s.7.

PART V

PROCEDURE AND ENFORCEMENT

5.1   Where an order is sought under the Domestic Violence and
Matrimonial Proceedings Act 1976 or under other powers of the High
Court and county courts the applicant has to serve notice of the
application for the injunction together with affidavit evidence and
any other relevant documents giving the required notice of the
hearing.[1] The period of notice required varies depending on the
jurisdiction.[2]

Emergency situations

5.2   Where it is necessary to take urgent action, frequently the
case in situations of severe domestic friction and violence, an
application can be made on affidavit evidence without prior notice to
the respondent.[3] An ex parte order will only be of very short
duration, until the earliest date when a hearing on notice can be
arranged.[4] In Ansah v Ansah it was said that:

> "Orders made ex parte are anomalies in our system of justice
> which generally demands service or notice of the proposed
> proceedings on the opposite party...Nontheless, the power of the

---

1. See Craig v. Kanssen [1943] K.B. 256, 262.

2. 21 days under the Matrimonial Homes Act 1983, 4 days under the
   Domestic Violence and Matrimonial Proceedings Act 1976, 2 days if
   ancillary to divorce proceedings; C.C.R., O.3 r.4, O.47 r.8, and
   O.13 r.1 respectively.

3. R.S.C., O.29, r. 1; C.C.R., O.13, r.6(3).

4. Ansah v. Ansah [1977] Fam. 138.

court to intervene immediately and without notice in proper cases is essential to the administration of justice."[5]

A Practice Note issued in 1978 states that:

"ex parte applications should not be made or granted unless there is a real immediate danger of serious injury or irreparable damage."[6]

5.3   The Practice Note does not distinguish between molestation and ouster.   In principle, however, the former does little more than restrain the respondent from breaking the law; but the latter involves (unless the respondent is trespassing on the applicant's premises) a balancing exercise which is difficult to carry out without at least the opportunity of an inter partes hearing.[7]   Nonetheless, while it may be necessary to restrict ex parte ouster orders to cases in which there is a real and immediate danger of harm if the respondent remains in or returns to the home pending the hearing, the requirement to show a risk of serious injury or irreparable damage places a heavy burden on an applicant, who might be thought entitled to pursue a remedy without running the risk of any injury.

5.4   Magistrates have power to grant expedited personal protection orders where there is imminent danger of physical injury to an applicant or child of the family.[8]   An expedited order may be made by a single justice and without any or the normal period of notice to the

---

[5]. Ibid. per Ormrod L.J.; see also Masich v. Masich (1977) 7 Fam.Law 245.

[6]. Practice Note (Matrimonial Cause: Injunctions) [1978] 1 W.L.R. 925.

[7]. See para. 3.8 et seq.

[8]. Domestic Proceedings and Magistrates' Courts Act 1978, s.16(6).

respondent.[9] An expedited order may only run for 28 days or until the substantive hearing, whichever is the sooner, and will not take effect until it is served on the other party or any later date specified by the court.[10] There is no power to make an expedited exclusion order, although there is power to relax other procedural requirements in both personal protection and exclusion cases if it is essential to hear them without delay.[11] Rules of court also provide that an application for exclusion should be heard as soon as possible and in any event not later than 14 days after issue of the summons.[12]

5.5   The fact that magistrates cannot make an expedited exclusion order means that it will often be preferable to seek an ex parte injunction in a county court. In those cases where an expedited order is necessary for personal protection it may well be that an exclusion order is also necessary to ensure the safety of the applicant or child.[13]

---

9. s.16(6) and (7).

10. s.16(8). Successive applications may be made by virtue of s.17(3).

11. Ibid., s.16(6) and (7). The court in such circumstances may hear an application notwithstanding that the court does not include both a man and a woman, that any member of the court is not a member of a domestic panel, or that the proceedings on the application are not separated from the hearing and determination of the proceedings which are not domestic proceedings.

12. See Domestic Proceedings and Magistrates' Courts Act 1978, s.17(2) and Magistrates' Courts (Matrimonial Proceedings) Rules 1980, SI 1980/1582 r.13(2).

13. In McCartney v. McCartney [1981] Fam. 59 it was said to be inconsistent to attach a power of arrest but refuse an exclusion order under the Domestic Proceedings and Magistrates' Courts Act 1978, s.16(3).

Enforcement

5.6   Breach of an injunction is not a criminal offence[14] although the facts of the breach may be relevant in a criminal prosecution.[15] However, failure to obey an injunction is a civil contempt and renders the respondent liable to committal to prison or a fine.[16] A contemnor may at any time seek to purge his contempt by ceasing his defiance and complying with the order, and so gain immediate release.[17] Because of the penal consequences it has to be shown beyond reasonable doubt that the defendant committed the breach.[18] When the court considers committal for breach of an injunction the following considerations will have to be balanced:

- the protection of the subject whose liberty is as stake;
- the complainant's right to be protected by the law against violence, threats and molestation;
- the welfare of any children;
- the authority of the courts in making and enforcing injunctions.[19]

---

14. It was said in Ansah v. Ansah [1977] Fam. 138, 144 per Ormrod L.J. that the court's real object where committing for contempt is "not so much to punish the disobedience as to secure compliance with the order in the future".

15. Where a criminal prosecution is brought the contempt proceedings should not be adjourned pending the outcome of the criminal proceedings. Szczepanski v. Szczepanski [1985] F.L.R. 468.

16. The maximum period of imprisonment is 2 years; Contempt of Court Act 1981, s.14(1).

17. Lightfoot v. Lightfoot [1989] 1 F.L.R. 414, (C.A.).

18. Dean v. Dean [1978] 3 All E.R. 758.

19. Wright v. Jess [1987] 1 W.L.R. 1076, 1083,4 per Bingham L.J.; in Brewer v. Brewer (1989) The Times, 17 Feb. (C.A.); it was held that an immediate committal to prison for the first breach of a matrimonial injunction was appropriate in exceptional cases only. A court would normally find it sufficient to make the committal order and then suspend it. However, in Lightfoot v. Lightfoot [1989] 1 F.L.R. 414, Mesham v. Clarke (1989) Fam.Law 192, it was

5.7   Both the High Court and county courts have powers to commit for contempt of court. Application is made to the court whose order has been breached. As punishment for contempt of court may result in committal to prison the procedural formalities and requirements of the law must be strictly complied with. According to Sir John Donaldson M.R.:

> "The number of reported decisions of this court on the subject of committal for breach of injunctions confirms that this is a field of jurisprudence in which it is easy to make mistakes of a more or less technical nature."[20]

Rules of court require that an order cannot be enforced by committal unless a copy of that order has been personally served on the person against whom the order has been made stating both what is required of them and the consequences of failure to meet those requirements.[21] Where there has been a serious and flagrant breach of an injunction to which a power of arrest has been attached it is not wrong in principle to make an ex parte committal order, although activating the power of arrest might be a more appropriate way for the court to deal with the matter as the court would then be able to hear the full facts on an inter partes hearing before imposing sentence.[22]

---

19. Continued
held that were the contemnor was in continuing and wilful breach the maximum sentence of 2 years was appropriate.

20. Wright v. Jess [1987] 1 W.L.R. 1076, 1083.

21. R.S.C., O.52, r.3; C.C.R., O.29, r.1. The court is empowered to dispense with service if it thinks that it is just to do so or if the judge is satisfied that, pending such service, the person against whom it is sought has had notice either by being present when the order was made, or by being notified of the terms of the order whether by telephone, telegram or otherwise. See generally Nguyen v. Phung [1984] 5 F.L.R. 773; Williams v. Fawcett [1985] 1 W.L.R. 501; Wright v. Jess [1987] 1 W.L.R. 1076.

22. See Newman v. Benesch [1987] 1 F.L.R. 262.

5.8   Committal for contempt is not available in magistrates'
courts, although any deliberate frustration of the efforts of the
court to protect justice from interference would amount to the common
law offence of contempt.[23] However, magistrates have power to impose
penalties for breach of orders, in proceedings under section 63(3) of
the Magistrates' Courts Act 1980,[24] which may be instituted either on
complaint or by the court of its own motion.[25] Furthermore, where
there are reasonable grounds for believing that the respondent has
disobeyed the order, an arrest warrant can be issued on the
application of the applicant for the order,[26] and if arrested the
respondent can be remanded in custody or on bail[27] pending the section
63 proceedings.   There are no equivalent powers pending proceedings
for committal in county courts.[28]

Powers of arrest

5.9   The enforcement of an injunction in the conventional way by
seeking committal for contempt of court may involve delay at a time
when the applicant is most vulnerable to further attack. The Domestic
Violence and Matrimonial Proceedings Act 1976 broke new ground by
empowering either the High Court of the county court to attach a power

---

23. See e.g., Att.Gen. v. News Group Newspapers Ltd, [1988] 3 W.L.R.
    163. Common law contempt is punishable only by the High Court. R.
    v. Davies [1906] 1 K.B.32.

24. Being in default of an order may result in fines not in excess of
    £2,000 or £50 every day or imprisonment for a period not exceeding
    2 months or "until he has remedied his default".

25. Contempt of Court Act 1981, s.17.

26. Domestic Proceedings and Magistrates' Courts Act 1978, s.18(4);
    this does not apply if there is already a power of arrest attached
    to the order.

27. Magistrates' Courts Act 1980, ss.128, 129; the Bail Act 1976 does
    not apply to such remands.

28. Wright v. Jess [1987] 1 W.L.R. 1076.

of arrest to an injunction containing at least one of the following provisions:

(a) restraining the other party from using violence against the applicant; or

(b) restraining the other party from using violence against a child living with the applicant; or

(c) excluding the other party form the matrimonial home or from a specified area in which the matrimonial home is included.[29]

Provided that the injunction contains one of these provisions then a power of arrest may be attached in any proceedings between husband and wife or a man and woman who are living together with each other as such.[30] It is doubtful, however, whether this includes proceedings under the Matrimonial Homes Act which result in "orders" rather than injunctions, although the effect is the same. The court must, in all cases, be satisfied that the respondent has caused "actual bodily harm" to the applicant or child and is likely to do so again.[31]

5.10   A power of arrest may also be attached to orders made in proceedings under the Domestic Proceedings and Magistrates' Courts Act 1978 that the respondent:

(a) shall not use violence against the person of the applicant; or

---

29. s.2(1).

30. Lewis v. Lewis [1978] 1 All E.R. 729; no power of arrest can be attached to similar orders made in wardship proceedings between parents who have never married or lived together; Re G. (Wardship) (Jurisdiction: Power of Arrest) (1983) 4 F.L.R. 538.

31. s.2(1).

(b) shall not use violence against a child of the family; or

(c) shall not enter the matrimonial home.[32]

The court must also be satisfied that the respondent has "physically injured" the applicant or child. If there is a difference between physical injury and actual bodily harm,[33] the former probably requires more than the latter, which has been held to include psychological conditions as well as bruises, lacerations and other injuries.[34] A further minor discrepancy is that magistrates wishing to attach a power of arrest to an exclusion order will have not only to order the respondent to leave but also to prohibit him from returning.

5.11   Unless otherwise provided a power of arrest can be exercised for as long as the order to which it is attached is in force. However, a Practice Note has stated that the power of arrest should not be regarded as a routine measure, and that a time limit of three months should normally be imposed upon its operation.[35]

5.12   The power of arrest entitles any constable to arrest without a warrant a person whom he has reasonable cause for suspecting of being in breach of the order to which the power is attached.[36]   The respondent cannot therefore be arrested for forms of molestation other

---

32. s.18(1). The power of arrest was not recommended in the Law Commission Report nor was it in the original Bill. It was added at report stage of the House of Commons. Hansard (H.C.), 19 May 1978, vol. 950, cols. 1035-1041.

33. According to the Under-Secretary of State for the Home Department (Dr. Shirley Summerskill) the phrases mean the same. Hansard (H.C.), 19 May 1978, Vol. 950, col. 1040.

34. R. v. Miller [1954] 2 Q.B. 282.

35. Practice Note (Domestic Violence: Power of Arrest) [1981] 1 W.L.R. 27.

36. 1976 Act, s.2(3); 1978 Act, s.18(2).

than violence, or for threats, or for refusing to leave the home in defiance of a magistrates' order. The arrested person must be brought before a judge[37] (or, if the order was made in a magistrates' court, before a justice of the peace),[38] within 24 hours.[39]   If arrested under the Domestic Violence and Matrimonial Proceedings Act 1976, a judge cannot remand the respondent. If arrested under the Domestic Proceedings and Magistrates' Courts Act 1978, on the other hand, the court or a justice of the peace, is empowered to remand the respondent in custody or on bail.[40] Committal proceedings generally follow from the circumstances which gave rise to the respondent's arrest.   The decision whether to bring proceedings is generally left to the applicant, although the court may commit for contempt where there is sufficient proof, despite the absence of an application from the aggrieved party.[41] Similarly in a magistrates court, proceedings under the Magistrates' Court Act may ensue, either on complaint or of the court's own motion.[42]

5.13   Hence there is a significant difference between the two main Acts in the power to remand the respondent after his appearance in court following arrest.   Magistrates' courts are, of course, principally criminal courts and are accustomed to issuing arrest warrants and remanding arrested people in custody or on bail.

---

37. 1976 Act, s.2(4).

38. 1978 Act, s.18(3).

39. Leaving out Sunday, Christmas Day and Good Friday.

40. The provisions of the Bail Act 1976, so far as they relate to criminal proceedings, do not apply and the magistrates should take recognizances or fix the amount of recognizances so that they might be taken elsewhere. See Magistrates Courts Act 1980, s.119.

41. However, in Boylan v. Boylan (1980) 11 Fam. Law. 225, it was held that the court should not punish for contempt if the aggrieved party had no wish to support the application.

42. Magistrates' Courts Act 1980, s.63(3); Contempt of Court Act 1981, s.17.

Although the higher courts' powers to commit for contempt of their orders may result in an eventual fine or imprisonment, there is no precedent for empowering the civil courts to direct detention of a person prior to the determination of a committal hearing. An alternative might be to make magistrates' courts the venue for the enforcement of all orders to which a power of arrest has been attached, irrespective of the court by which the order was made.

5.14   Powers of arrest are attached to a relatively small proportion of injunctions,[43] no doubt because they are regarded as an exceptional matter. Yet the Select Committee had argued strongly that injunctions would not be properly enforced unless the police had this power.[44] It has therefore been suggested that a power of arrest should be attached in all cases involving violence unless the judge is satisfied that there is no danger of physical attack.[45]

5.15   A further criticism is that powers of arrest are not available between former spouses and people who are no longer living together as husband and wife.[46] There is often a particular need for protection in such cases. Also, any doubt about whether powers of arrest can be

---

[43] In 1987, under the 1978 Act, in about one third of the general applications and in about one half of the applications for expedited orders a power of arrest was attached. In the same year, under the 1976 Act, almost three tenths of all injunctions had powers of arrest attached. (Almost 70 per cent of the injunctions granted under the 1976 Act were for non-molestation.) See L. Smith, Domestic Violence: an overview of the literature, Home Office Research Study No. 107 (1989), p.14.

[44] Report from the Select Committee on Violence in Marriage (1974-75), H.C. 553-i, Vol.1. para.45.

[45] Women's National Commission, Violence against Women, Report of an ad hoc working group (1985), para. 113; there is evidence from the U.S.A. and Canada that arrest in cases of domestic violence prevents reoffending. See S. Torgbor, "Police Intervention in Domestic Violence – A Comparative View", [1989] Fam. Law 195.

[46] See para. 4.6 above.

attached to longer term orders excluding a violent respondent from the home in proceedings under the Matrimonial Homes Act could be resolved. If the power is appropriate and necessary in certain types of case, there should be no technical distinction between different types of proceeding.

Undertakings

5.16   An undertaking is an obligation volunteered to and accepted by the court. County courts will frequently accept an undertaking from the respondent in substitution for, and in the same terms as, an injunction that it would otherwise have granted. Despite its non-coercive appearance, an undertaking plays exactly the same role as an injunction, being enforceable by contempt proceedings. The giving of an undertaking enables the court to endorse a voluntary obligation not so strictly governed by procedural requirements which have to be complied with before it can be enforced.[47]

5.17   As the importance of ensuring that a respondent is fully aware of his obligations, before he is in peril of being imprisoned for failure to comply, applies just as much to undertakings as it does to injunctions, formal provision now exists in the county court for the judge to direct that the party making the undertaking sign an acknowledgement of his undertaking in court.[48] The standard of proof required to show that the respondent has broken his undertaking is the same as if there had been an injunction.

---

47. C.C.R., O.29, r.1 has no direct application to cases of committal for breach of an undertaking: Hussain v. Hussain [1986] 1 All E.R. 961. According to Sir John Donaldson M.R., "it is the undertaking and not the order which requires the giver of the undertaking to act in accordance with its terms"; thus technically, the order does not have to be endorsed with a penal notice and personally served on the respondent before he can be committed.

48. County Court (Forms)(Amendments) Rules 1988, S.I. 1988/279.

5.18   Although undertakings are a common substitute for injunctions in county courts they are not used formally in magistrates' courts, as they cannot be enforced. Indeed neither the terminology of injunction nor undertaking is used by magistrates; the term order is always used. If magistrates were to be empowered to accept undertakings in proceedings under the Domestic Proceedings and Magistrates' Court Act 1978, they might be given the same power to punish for non-compliance as they have for breach of a court order.

5.19   There is no power to attach a power of arrest to an undertaking.[49] To give such a power might destroy the principal benefit of undertakings, which is to attract the authority of the court without a fully fledged hearing of all the issues. It is not necessary for the person giving the undertaking to admit the truth of any allegations or that they constitute a good case for the exercise of the court's discretion. The imposition of a police power to arrest without warrant might not be thought appropriate without a trial or admission that the statutory grounds existed.

[49.] _Carpenter_ v. _Carpenter_ [1988] 1 F.L.R. 121.

PART VI

APPROACHES TO REFORM

6.1   The previous parts have identified numerous inconsistencies between the various provisions, together with gaps and deficiencies in the protection afforded. The options for reform fall into two broad categories:

    (1) retain the basic structure of the present law but seek to remove as many inconsistencies, gaps and deficiencies as possible; or

    (2) restructure the law so as to provide a single, consistent set of remedies, with or without variations between -different courts.

To a large extent, the feasibility of the second option depends upon how many of the individual reforms contemplated under the first are thought acceptable or desirable. We should therefore welcome views on each of the possibilities canvassed below.

(1)   Individual reforms

(i)   The people protected

(a)   Former spouses

6.2   It appears that former spouses may still be protected against molestation but that, for the most part, the power to grant ouster and regulate occupation ends at decree absolute.[1] Three minor reforms or

---

[1.] See paras. 4.2-4.6 above.

clarifications seem worthy of consideration. First, the existing
power to regulate occupation rights between spouses who are joint
owners or tenants[2] could be extended to all cases where the parties
were married to one another when or after the home was acquired, even
if they have subsequently been divorced. Secondly, where only one is
the legal owner or tenant, but a court has already ordered that the
non-owner's rights of occupation should continue after the divorce,[3]
it should be made clear that the court continues to have the same
power to resolve disputes as it had before, including a power to oust
the owning spouse. Thirdly, if the non-owner has applied for a
property adjustment[4] or transfer of tenancy order,[5] the same power to
resolve disputes about occupation could continue until that
application was resolved.

(b)   Cohabitants

6.3   People who are currently living together as husband and wife
can be protected against molestation, but not those whose relationship
ended before the events leading to the application.[6] Yet former
cohabitants may have just as much need as have former spouses for a
simple remedy, which does not require them to launch an ordinary
action in tort and which may, on occasions, protect them from
harassing behaviour which is not always covered by the law of tort.[7]

---

2. Matrimonial Homes Act 1983, s.9.

3. 1983 Act, s.2(4).

4. Under Matrimonial Causes Act 1973, s.24.

5. Under 1983 Act, s.7 and sched.1.

6. See paras. 4.7-4.8 above.

7. See para. 4.12 above.

6.4   As to disputes about occupation and ouster, cases such as
Ainsbury v. Millington[8] suggest that there is a need, at the very
least, to extend the courts' power to regulate occupation rights
between spouses who are joint owners or tenants, under section 9 of
the Matrimonial Homes Act 1983, to joint owners or tenants who are or
have been living together as husband and wife.   It could be argued
that this power already extends to couples who have been engaged to
marry, by virtue of section 2(1) of the Law Reform (Miscellanelous
Provisions) Act 1970, which applies to such couples any rule of law
relating to the property of husband and wife.[9] Such a reform would be
consistent with, but rather more limited than, the Commission's recent
recommendation that the courts should have extensive powers to resolve
disputes relating to land held on trust, as all jointly owned land
must be.[10]

6.5   Where such cohabitants are not jointly entitled to occupy, any
remedy designed to protect the occupation of the non-entitled party
must at present be of relatively short duration.[11]   While the "three
month" guideline may be too restrictive, it might be helpful to set a
maximum so as to clarify the position for all.   However, the
Matrimonial Homes (Family Protection) (Scotland) Act 1981, goes
further, and allows the court to grant a non-entitled cohabitant
"occupancy rights" like those automatically given to spouses,
initially for up to three months but thereafter renewable for periods
of up to six months at a time.[12] The advantage of this approach is
that it can attract the provisions of the Matrimonial Homes Act which

---

8. [1986] 1 All E.R. 73; see para. 4.9 above.

9. See Mossop v. Mossop [1988] 2 W.L.R. 1255.

10. Trusts of Land (1989), Law Com. No.181, paras. 12.6-12.13.

11. See paras. 3.32-3.34 above.

12. s.18.

empower the court to make ancillary orders about repairs and outgoings[13] and, perhaps more importantly, equate the occupation and discharge of outgoings by the non-entitled spouse with that of the entitled.[14] The landlord or mortgagee is thus in the same position as if the entitled spouse had remained in the home and continued to pay the rent or mortgage instalments now being paid by the occupant. In cases where there is no security of tenure it remains open to the landlord to terminate the letting or licence if he so wishes. The Domestic Violence and Matrimonial Proceedings Act 1976 makes no provision for these matters, whereas the Scottish legislation does so.

6.6   Where there is statutory security of tenure, the effect of a spouse's rights of occupation is to prevent the landlord regaining possession simply because the entitled spouse leaves or surrenders the tenancy.[15] (Paradoxically, where they are joint tenants, it appears that one can bring a secure tenancy to an end by surrender.[16]) On or after divorce, nullity or judicial separation, the court therefore has power to transfer a protected, statutory, secure or assured tenancy from one spouse to the other or from them both to one alone.[17] The advantage of extending a similar power where cohabitation comes to an end would be to provide a permanent solution to cases such as Ainsbury v. Millington,[18] where a secure tenancy was granted to a couple who had since ceased their relationship and neither the court nor the local authority had any power to decide which of them should continue in occupation. The landlord is entitled to be heard in the transfer

---

13. s.1(3); see paras. 3.2-3.5 above and 6.18 below.

14. s.1(5)-(8).

15. Middleton v. Baldock [1950] 1 K.B. 657; see para. 2.4 above.

16. London Borough of Greenwich v. McGrady (1983) 81 L.G.R. 288; see para. 3.13 above.

17. Matrimonial Homes Act 1983, s.7 and sched. 1; extended to assured tenancies by virtue of Housing Act 1988, sched. 17, para.34.

18. [1986] 1 All E.R. 73; see para. 4.9 above.

proceedings, so that he can voice any objections to one of the couple taking over the tenancy.[19] Further, although when the court regulates occupation it may also regulate payment of outgoings, this can only operate between the parties, and it could be unjust and undesirable to deprive a tenant of occupation rights for any length of time while leaving him liable to the landlord should the occupier default.[20] On the other hand, what may be appropriate in the context of a global financial settlement on divorce may not be so where no such possibility exists.[21]

6.7   An alternative solution, at least in relation to council tenancies,[22] would be to give an additional ground to local authorities seeking possession. This might be to the effect that the family relationship between the tenants had broken down and the authority wished to transfer the tenancy to one of them.[23] This would leave the decision as to which was the more "deserving" to the local authority. The present criteria applied by the courts under the Matrimonial Homes Act appear considerably more tender to the needs of the adult who is not responsible for the care of any children than a

---

19. 1983 Act, sched. 1, para. 8; it would appear that these provisions apply notwithstanding any covenant against assignment; cf. the court's powers under section 24 Matrimonial Causes Act 1973, which apply to "property"; quaere whether a tenancy containing a covenant against assignment can be "property"; see Hale v. Hale [1975] 1 W.L.R. 931; Thompson v. Thompson [1976] Fam. 25; Regan v. Regan [1977] 1 W.L.R. 84.

20. See e.g. Griffiths v. Renfree, The Times, 4 March 1989 (C.A.) where a husband was found liable to the landlord even though he had given notice because occupation by the wife was treated as occupation by the husband under a statutory tenancy.

21. There may be occasions in which the transfer of a tenancy would deprive one party of entitlement to large sums, for example because of a right to buy. The inability to compensate for this should no doubt be relevant to the exercise of the court's discretion.

22. "Marital dispute" was the primary reason for homelessness accepted by local authorities for almost 20% of those housed by local authorities in 1987. Homeless Households Accepted by Local Authorities in England and Wales 1987, Department of the Environment.

local authority can afford to be. It is usually the needs of the children which have led to the allocation of the tenancy in the first place. However, as the decision between married partners is currently left to the matrimonial jurisdiction, there is a case for doing the same with unmarried partners.

6.8   A further change which could be considered is to give magistrates' courts power to grant personal protection or exclusion orders to cohabitants as well as spouses, whether or not those powers remain limited to cases of violence.[24] Exclusion orders give rise to more complex questions than simple personal protection, but only in some cases. Ironically, the simplest case is where the couple are joint owners or tenants, which is not covered by the present law but gives rise to questions of merit rather than law. The most meritorious case may be that of an applicant who is the sole owner or tenant, for whom a simple remedy to protect rights of occupation and oust the other partner in a magistrates' court would no doubt be helpful. Even the cohabitant without a legal right to occupy might be permitted to claim short term relief as is already available in county courts. The difficulty in cases of apparent sole ownership, whether of applicant or respondent, is that the other may claim to have a beneficial interest and with it the right to occupy. It is scarcely reasonable to expect magistrates to resolve such questions. But they might be enabled to give short term relief in any event, while the appropriate proceedings are launched elsewhere.

6.9   Unfortunately, "elsewhere" in so many property disputes between cohabitants has to be the High Court, even though the issues are no different from those which were for many years resolved in

---

23. As is provided in Scotland; see Housing (Scotland) Act 1986, s.11, adding para. 6 to Schedule 2 to the Tenants' Rights, Etc.(Scotland) Act 1980.

24. See para. 4.11 above.

county courts (indeed by registrars) under section 17 of the Married Women's Property Act 1882. Although somewhat outside the scope of this project, it is worth considering whether such cases might be begun (as well as heard) in county courts, where they could be consolidated with molestation and occupation cases. One way of doing this would be to extend section 17 to cohabitants.[25] No breach of principle would be involved as that section does not alter the parties' respective property rights under the general law. It has already been extended to engaged couples.[26] In the present social climate it is difficult to justify imposing a more costly procedure for determining the same type of dispute upon those who have not agreed to marry. It is often difficult in practice to distinguish between them.

(c)   Other family members

6.10   The strains which give rise to remedies against molestation between spouses and cohabitants may also occur between other family members, but at present they have no right to protection against harassment unless it falls within the torts of assault, battery, trespass or nuisance.[27] The law does recognise a special need to protect tenants and debtors from harassment by their landlords and creditors,[28] and reported cases supply considerable evidence that a similar need is felt between members of a family.[29] It would,

---

25. Section 17 provides as follows: In any question between husband and wife as to the title to or possession of property, either party, may apply by summons or otherwise in a summary way to the High Court or such county court as may be prescribed and the court may, on such an application (which may be heard in private), make such order with respect to the property as it thinks fit.

26. Law Reform (Miscellaneous Provisions) Act 1970, s.2(2).

27. See para. 4.12-4.13 above.

28. Protection from Eviction Act 1977, s.1; Administration of Justice Act 1970, s.40.

29. See cases cited at para. 2.16, n.46.

however, be difficult to define the class to which such a remedy might apply, whether by reference to permanent relationships or to membership of a common household, as well as the scope of the behaviour involved. It may also be undesirable to encourage people to come to court with minor allegations of molestation (or indeed other unlawful behaviour).[30] Nevertheless, within the family there can be the same inhibitions against taking much needed legal action as exist between husband and wife.

(d)   Children

6.11   As to the children who can be protected against molestation, a simple reform would be to resolve the discrepancy between the county courts' powers to protect any child "living with" the applicant and magistrates' courts' powers to protect only children of the family.[31] Strictly, protection for children involved in divorce proceedings may also be limited to children of the family, while the Matrimonial Homes Act criteria refer to the needs of "any children". Given that this protection is normally ancillary to protection for adults, there may be no need for any restriction by relationship. Alternatively, it could refer to any child of, or living with, either party.

6.12   The case of Tuck v. Nicholls[32] suggests that there may occasionally be a need, similar to that in Ainsbury v. Millington,[33] to regulate occupation rights, especially of council houses, between joint tenants who are parents but who have never married or lived together. It appears anomalous that where a joint council tenancy has been granted to a couple with a baby, but only one has yet moved in,

---

30. See Patel v. Patel [1988] 2 F.L.R. 179, 182 per May L.J.

31. See paras. 4.14-4.16 above.

32. [1989] 1 F.L.R. 283.

33. [1986] 1 All E.R. 73.

no-one should have power in the event of a breakdown of their relationship to decide which of them should be allowed to occupy it. Once again, a power to transfer the tenancy itself might be a better long term solution than the power to adjust occupation rights.[34] It might also be helpful to allow parents and others with parental responsibility for a child to seek remedies against molestation by another parent without having to bring proceedings about the child's care or upbringing.

6.13 The most radical reform, however, would be to introduce powers to make non-molestation and, more importantly, ouster orders to protect children who are at risk of abuse.[35] We would particularly welcome views about whether such powers are needed and, if so, whether they would be best integrated with the private law remedies under discussion in this paper or the public law remedies against child abuse provided in the Children Bill now before Parliament. The subject is further discussed in Appendix A.

(e)   Application on another's behalf

6.14 It has apparently proved valuable in some states in Australia to enable the police, or any person authorised by the victim, to bring proceedings on the victim's behalf.[36] It requires considerable courage and determination on the part of the victims of domestic violence to bring proceedings against an attacker. Such powers could take one burden off the victims' shoulders, although as the remedy is designed for their benefit, the victims' co-operation and agreement would be essential. The process would represent a further intrusion by the police into matters of civil law, although the results might be

---

34. See para. 6.6 above.

35. See paras. 4.18–4.19 above.

36. See para. 4.20 above.

more welcome and useful to the victim than the process of prosecution
and punishment.

(ii)   The scope and duration of remedies

(a)   Molestation

6.15   It might be thought desirable in principle to provide a
statutory definition of the types of behaviour covered by
"molestation",[37] so that the person enjoined knows exactly what is
prohibited and the approach of the courts is consistent.   Against
this, the types of behaviour involved in molestation are many and
various, and their impact depends upon the past history, the
surrounding circumstances and the motive of the molester.   There is
little evidence of any difficulty arising in practice, although some
courts prefer to use the more everyday terms "harass or interfere"
rather than "molest".

6.16   There might be a stronger case for defining molestation if the
concept were also to be employed in magistrates' courts.   At present,
magistrates are only empowered to grant protection against the use or
threat of "violence".[38]   In 1976, it was thought that other forms of
molestation involved "psychological harm" and thus the assessment of
expert evidence which magistrates would find difficult.[39]   In reality,
however, molestation cases are of two main types.   In the first, there
has been violence in the past, and menacing behaviour such as banging
on doors, hanging about the area or other places where the applicant
goes, or frequent telephone calls, causes the applicant to fear it
again.   In the second, such behaviour indicates an unwillingness to

---

37.   See paras. 3.26-3.28 above.

38.   See paras. 3.29-3.30 above.

39.   (1976) Law Com. No.77, para. 3.12.

"let go" which can seriously disturb the peace of mind and way of life of the applicant and the children. Even if the grounds upon which magistrates can make orders remain limited to the use or threat of violence, the orders themselves might prohibit a wider range of harassing behaviour. The issues involved are no more difficult than those which arise in binding over or the less serious public order offences.[40]

(b)　　　Exclusion from area or part of home

6.17　　Another possible reform would be to remove the discrepancies between the various Acts[41] and allow all courts to exclude, not only from the family home itself, but also from a specified area in which the home is included or from part only of the home. The power to exclude from the street, estate or block of flats is an extremely useful way of specifying one form of unacceptable molestation. The power to exclude from part of the home is particularly valuable where some of it is used for business, but also where the essential need is to find a way in which an estranged couple can continue to share the only premises available to them for what is usually a transitional period before total separation or reconciliation. There is little reason to preserve the discrepancies between the powers of the higher courts under the Domestic Violence and Matrimonial Proceedings Act 1976 and the Matrimonial Homes Act 1983 in this respect.[42] Against extending such powers to magistrates, it could be said that exclusion from an area is a powerful weapon to be used with caution and that dividing up the house is unlikely to be a practical solution in the cases which come before the magistrates' courts. The issues involved are nevertheless no more complex than others with which magistrates

---

40. E.g. the offences of intimidating, persistently following, watching or besetting under the Conspiracy and Protection of Property Act 1875, s.7.

41. See paras. 3.2-3.5 above.

42. Para. 3.2-3.3 above.

75

regularly deal. Differences of this nature perpetuate the criticism that there is one law for those who apply to the higher courts and another for those, predominantly from the poorer sections of society, who apply to the magistrates' courts.

(c)   <u>Ancillary orders</u>

6.18   At present, it is only possible to make ancillary orders about the discharge of rent, mortgage instalments or other outgoings in proceedings under the Matrimonial Homes Act.[43] This is one reason why it may be desirable that orders under the Domestic Violence Act, even between parties who are jointly entitled, are of relatively short duration. Relieving the ousted party of the obligation to pay rent may not only defuse tension but also be a useful first step towards setting up distinct households. Such orders do not, of course, bind landlords or mortgagees, who are still entitled to take appropriate action if the debt is not paid. Further, in some emergency cases, there may not be time to investigate the parties' respective financial liabilities and resources and the principal relief should not be delayed while this is done. Nonetheless, the power would be a useful one in some cases. The Matrimonial Homes Act also makes it clear that tender of outgoings by a spouse (whether or not under such an order) is a good discharge of the liability;[44] we have already suggested that similar provision might be made for cohabitants during the period of their occupation.[45]

6.19   Under the Matrimonial Homes Act there is power to order the non-entitled spouse to make payments for occupation.[46] It is unlikely

---

43. Para. 3.2 above.

44. s.1(5).

45. Para. 6.5 above.

46. s.1(3)(b).

that this is much used, given that the non-entitled spouse is unlikely to have the resources both to discharge the outgoings and to compensate the owner. Her possession of the home will normally go some way to discharge the other's obligations to maintain the family. In principle, however, if such a power is permissible between spouses (however rarely used) it is a fortiori permissible between cohabitants, who have no mutual duties to provide for one another. Once again, however, the short term of the order, together with the parties' resources, will usually make this impracticable.

6.20   There is no power under the 1976 or 1983 Acts to make orders about the use of furniture, whereas magistrates may be able to attach conditions to this effect under the 1978 Act.[47]   There is also power to do this in Scotland.[48] A similar power might be useful here.[49]

(d)   Re-entry orders in magistrates' courts

6.21   In the 1976 Report, the Commission recommended against giving magistrates' courts powers to enforce the non-entitled spouse's rights of occupation under the Matrimonial Homes Act.[50] This was principally because of advice[51] that that Act was not used in cases involving domestic violence, advice which can no longer hold good in the light of Richards v. Richards.[52]   In any event, a power to order the respondent to permit the applicant to re-enter the home was inserted

---

[47.] s. 16(9).

[48.] Matrimonial Home (Family Protection)(Scotland) Act 1981, s.3(2).

[49.] See also Third Report on Family Property. The Matrimonial Home (Co-Ownership and Occupation Rights) and Household Goods (1978), Law Com. No.82.

[50.] (1976) Law Com. No.77, paras. 3.26-3.27.

[51.] From Sir George Baker, then President of the Family Division.

[52.] [1984] A.C.174; para. 3.6 et seq. above.

in the Domestic Proceedings and Magistrates' Courts Act, but only where the respondent was himself excluded.[53] Once again, if the magistrates' powers remain limited to violence, there may be little point in enforcing re-entry while permitting the respondent to remain. It is, however, not uncommon for a spouse to be locked out of the house after an argument and to need a quick remedy to get back in for the sake of the children who remain, whether or not the more drastic remedy of ouster is called for. If magistrates are thought able to impose the more drastic remedy, it is difficult to see why they should not be thought able to enforce the right which each spouse has at common law and by statute to occupy the matrimonial home.

6.22 More difficult issues might arise if magistrates' powers were to be extended to cohabitants. Here again, however, if the cohabitant who has been locked out has a right to occupy, it would not give rise to serious questions of principle if the magistrates were to be permitted to enforce that right. Even if he or she does not, if the court is to be given power (in certain circumstances or for a limited period) to exclude the one who is entitled, it is not obviously wrong to give a power to permit re-entry instead of, rather than simply as well as, exclusion.

(e) Duration

6.23 In principle, orders restraining molestation or violence, or regulating rights of occupation between people who are both entitled to occupy (which includes all spouses), should be capable of lasting as long as they are needed. This will obviously vary with the circumstances, and in some cases short term relief will be all that is necessary or appropriate. Nevertheless, the "three month" guidance

---

53. s.16(4).

78

may have been misinterpreted or appear to lay down too inflexible a rule.[54]

6.24   Where the applicant for ouster or re-entry is not entitled to occupy, a time limit is more realistic. As we have already seen,[55] in Scotland the limit for non-entitled cohabitants is up to three months in the first instance, but renewable for periods of up to six months at a time.   It might therefore be desirable to prescribe some such limit, thus enabling the guidance which may be applied in inappropriate cases at present to be rescinded.

(iii)   Criteria for orders

6.25   The most difficult and important questions arise with the criteria for orders. The remedies provided by family law are designed to protect and support the physically and economically more vulnerable members of the family.   At the same time, the aim is to avoid unnecessary bitterness and conflict, and in particular to discourage prolonged arguments about who is most to blame for the unhappy differences which have arisen between the parties.   It is not easy to reconcile these aims in molestation and ouster cases.   The criteria should be sufficiently flexible and sensitive to ensure that protection is given to those who need it, but without encouraging people in the early stages of relationship breakdown to come to court to solve any and every dispute about their living arrangements.   When couples do come to court, the aim so far as possible should be to defuse rather than to exacerbate tensions.   Yet it can be hard to do this while ensuring swift and effective protection against violence.

[54.] See paras. 3.32-3.37 above.

[55.] Para. 6.5 above.

(a)   Anti-molestation orders

6.26   No statutory criteria exist for granting anti-molestation
injunctions, other than the general principle that it must be "just
and convenient" to do so, but in Spindlow v. Spindlow[56] it was said
that there must be some real evidence of molestation. Given the wide
range of behaviour involved and the variety of circumstances which can
arise, it would be difficult to devise a criterion which covered every
case while giving real help to the courts. A possibility might be
that such an order ought to be granted in the interests of the health,
safety or well-being of the applicant or child concerned.[57]

(b)   Ouster and occupation

6.27   The criteria for ouster in the higher courts are now those in
the Matrimonial Homes Act, together with the recent emphasis on the
draconian nature of such orders.[58] We have already seen that the
three main criticisms which have been made of these criteria are,
first, that they fail to take account of the very different types of
case in which orders may be sought; secondly, that at least as later
interpreted and applied, they seem to give too much weight to relative
blameworthiness compared with other factors; and thirdly, that they
give insufficient weight to the interests of children.

6.28   The first question is whether the criteria should refer at all
to the way in which the parties have behaved or the reason why one of
them feels unable to live with the other. On the one hand is the view
taken since Richards, that the respondent's conduct must be bad enough

---

56. [1979] Fam. 52.

57. This is similar to the criterion thought by Lord Scarman to be
     appropriate for non-molestation orders under the 1976 Act in
     Richards v. Richards [1984] A.C. 174, 208.

58. Paras. 3.6 et seq.

to justify the consequences to him of having to leave. On the other is the view taken in many of the cases before that, that what was just and reasonable depended on the "application of ordinary common sense to the circumstances before the court", and that generally speaking at least, "it is no good taking up a great deal of time talking in terms of blame or conduct".[59] In none of those cases, however, were the circumstances of the parting (or proposed parting) actually ignored.[60] A middle course, which accords with many of the decisions in fact reached, would be to require that in all the circumstances of the case, it was, for the time being or indefinitely, not reasonable to expect the parties to continue living in the same house.[61] This would enable the court to deny the remedy to an obviously unmeritorious applicant, who had no real reason for living apart or was merely seeking to improve her position in eventual property adjustment proceedings, while taking account both of the problems of those who need personal protection and the disadvantages of requiring full-blown trials of the parties' conduct pending divorce.

6.29   No criticism has been made of the requirement to consider the parties' respective needs and resources. This may simply be another way of expressing what was termed in the earlier cases the "balance of hardship" between them.[62] The "balance of hardship" test has two advantages over the present approach of the courts. First, it recognises that an ouster order will frequently have a severe or draconian effect, but obliges the court to consider how great, in the

---

59. <u>Spindlow</u> v. <u>Spindlow</u> [1979] Fam.52, 60 <u>per</u> Ormrod L.J.

60. <u>Bassett</u> v. <u>Bassett</u> [1975] Fam. 76; <u>Walker</u> v. <u>Walker</u> [1978] 1 W.L.R. 533; <u>Hopper</u> v. <u>Hopper</u> [1978] 1 W.L.R. 1342; <u>Spindlow</u> v. <u>Spindlow</u> [1979] Fam 52, 61 <u>per</u> Lawton L.J.

61. This can be distinguished from the test in the ground for divorce, which is that the <u>respondent has behaved</u> in such a way that the petitioner cannot be expected to live with him; Matrimonial Causes Act 1973 s1(2)(b).

62. See <u>Bassett</u> v. <u>Bassett</u> [1975] Fam. 76.

particular case, the hardship to the respondent will in fact be. Secondly, it obliges the court to compare the hardship likely to be caused by making the order with the hardship likely to be caused by refusing it. In both cases, the hardship caused to any children involved, whether by the making or the refusing of the order, can also be considered.

6.30   As for the needs of any children, Lord Scarman in Richards v. Richards argued that:

> "When an ouster is sought in pending divorce proceedings, the court is being invited to intervene at a most critical period in the lives of the children, the relationship between their parents having broken down (possibly irretrievably). The court is seized with the question of their welfare and upbringing. If ever there was a time to apply the principle of paramountcy of their welfare and upbringing, it is in pending divorce proceedings."[63]

Even in other cases, he argued, the question of ouster could not be considered without regard to the issue of their future, where again their welfare should be paramount.

6.31   In cases where the welfare of the children is paramount, it has been held that it "rules upon or determines the course to be followed."[64] This is universally accepted where the decision relates directly to who is to look after them or how they are to be brought up, but not where the interests of adults are equally involved. The effect of Richards appears to have been that the interests of an adult in remaining in the home must prevail unless his behaviour has been so

---

63. [1984] A.C. 174, 212.

64. J. v. C. [1970] A.C. 668, 711 per Lord MacDermott.

bad as to justify the consequences to him, which clearly makes the interests of adults paramount over those of the children. A middle course could be to provide that the children's interests should come first but not necessarily paramount over all others. This would accord with recent precedents in the law relating to financial provision and property adjustment.[65]

6.32   It is the general policy of the law to emphasise the responsibilities of parents towards their children and to put their interests first in all decisions relating to the family. If the parents knew that the children's interests would come first in any decision about occupation of the home it might encourage a more pragmatic and resolute attempt at solving problems of accommodation without self-interested recourse to litigation. The real difficulty is whether courts can effectively be required to give greater priority to the interests of children without making their interests paramount. Thus it has been forcefully argued that to make a factor the court's "first" consideration is useless, as it gives no indication of its relative weight.[66]

6.33   We find it difficult to improve upon the "balance of hardship" test, which was described by Cumming-Bruce L.J. in the case of <u>Bassett</u> v. <u>Bassett</u> as follows:

> "I extract from the cases the principle that the court will consider with care the accommodation available to both spouses, and the hardship to which each will be exposed if an order is granted or refused, and then consider whether it is really sensible to expect [the applicant] and child to endure the

---

[65]. Matrimonial Causes Act 1973, s.25(1); Domestic Proceedings and Magistrates' Courts Act 1978, s.3(1).

[66]. F. Bennion, "First Consideration: A Cautionary Tale" (1976) 126 N.L.J. 1237.

pressures which the continued presence of the other spouse will place on them. Obviously inconvenience is not enough. Equally obviously, the court must be alive to the risk that a spouse may be using the instrument of an injunction as a tactical weapon in the matrimonial conflict... Where there are children, whom the [applicant] is looking after, a major consideration must be to relieve them of the psychological stresses and strains imposed by the friction between their parents, as the long-term effect on a child is liable to be of the utmost gravity."[67]

(c) Magistrates' courts

6.34   Magistrates' courts at present can only act where there is the use or threat of violence.[68] To widen their scope to other forms of molestation might encourage people to resort to court over very trivial matters unless some other criterion, such as a likelihood of physical or mental harm, were added. On the other hand, the issues involved in granting protection against molestation do not cause serious problems in practice at present and are no different in kind from many others dealt with by magistrates.

6.35   Traditionally, magistrates' courts have not dealt with property-related matters.[69] We would not seek to alter this. Regulating rights of occupation can, however, be distinguished from determining rights of property. The former requires an exercise of the court's discretion in the light of factors (such as the parties'

---

[67]. Bassett v. Bassett [1975] Fam. 76, 87.

[68]. See paras. 3.17-3.18 and 3.29, above.

[69]. E.g. property adjustment orders for the benefit of children and orders relating to the management of children's property are excluded from their powers under the Guardianship of Minors Act 1971 and from the replacement powers in the Children Bill now before Parliament.

needs and resources and the needs of their children) which is similar
to that involved in the assessment of financial provision.[70]   If
magistrates are able to decide how much one party should pay the
other, they may equally be able to decide which of them should occupy
the home, at least for the time being.   Questions of title to property
do not arise between married couples, who are both entitled to occupy
the matrimonial home.   As between unmarried couples, we have already
seen that questions of right to occupy may depend upon difficult
questions of beneficial ownership. _ We would not expect magistrates to
resolve the latter, although they might be empowered to give short
term occupation remedies until proceedings are determined elsewhere.
Generally, however, the questions involved in resolving disputes about
occupation between equally entitled people are different in kind from
the questions involved in determining title to property.

(iv)   Powers of arrest

(a)   Orders to which powers of arrest may be attached

6.36   There is some doubt as to whether powers of arrest can be
attached to "orders" in proceedings under the Matrimonial Homes Act as
opposed to "injunctions" in matrimonial proceedings or under the
Domestic Violence Act.[71]   As the substantive law applicable is
identical, there seems no good reason to discriminate according to the
type of proceedings in which the order is made.

6.37   Powers of arrest can only be attached in proceedings between
spouses or people living together as husband and wife.[72]   Yet former
spouses or cohabitants may be in just as much need of the protection

---

[70]. See Domestic Proceedings and Magistrates' Courts Act 1978, s.3(2).

[71]. See para. 5.9 above.

[72]. See para. 4.6. above.

they afford as are current spouses and cohabitants. A further possibility would be to extend them to orders against violence made in other family proceedings;[73] this would enable powers of arrest to be attached to such orders in wardship or proceedings under the Guardianship of Minors Act without the need for separate proceedings under the 1976 Act and also, perhaps, between parties who had never been married or lived together. There is no difference in principle between these cases and those already covered by the Act.

(b)   The criteria

6.38   At present, it is necessary to show both that the respondent has caused actual bodily harm (or physical injury) in the past and that he is likely to do so again. It has been suggested that injunctions against violence should normally carry a power of arrest, unless this can be shown to be unnecessary.[74] In Scotland, the court is bound to attach a power of arrest (if asked) to any matrimonial interdict which is ancillary to an exclusion order. It must also attach a power to any other matrimonial interdict granted after the respondent has had an opportunity of being heard, unless this appears unnecessary in all the circumstances.[75] The criteria for granting both exclusion orders and interdicts in Scotland may be more limited than in England and Wales, but the criteria for imposing powers of arrest appear considerably less so.

6.39   The assumption that ouster cases must necessarily be so serious that powers of arrest should always be added to an

---

[73.] Cf. Re G. (Wardship)(Jurisdiction: Power of Arrest) (1983) 4 F.L.R. 538.

[74.] Women's National Commission, Violence against Women, Report of an ad hoc Working Group (1985), para.113.

[75.] Matrimonial Homes (Family Protection)(Scotland) Act 1981, s.15(1)(a) and (b) respectively.

accompanying order to keep away may be counter-productive. It may be more important that the courts are prepared to grant ouster where this is the sensible solution to the family's housing problems than that findings of violence are made which inevitably lead to a further serious consequence for the person ousted. A middle course could be to provide that, where actual bodily harm has been caused, a power of arrest should be attached to any order restraining violence, excluding from the home or area, or restraining re-entry, unless it appears that the applicant or child will be adequately protected without it. Against this, many will see powers of arrest as a sanction of last resort which can only exacerbate tensions unless they are reserved for cases where they can be shown to be necessary to provide protection against a risk of future harm.[76] In any event, the discrepancy between the "actual bodily harm" which suffices in the higher courts and the "physical injury" which must be shown in magistrates' courts could be removed.[77]

(c)   Remand

6.40   There is an important distinction between the powers of county and magistrates' courts once the respondent has been arrested.[78] In a county court, the respondent cannot be detained after his appearance in court unless the court has on that occasion found him guilty of contempt and committed him to prison. Yet it may be impossible to do this so quickly, perhaps because the applicant is too upset to take matters further immediately to prove the breach or because the respondent requires an opportunity to be legally represented. Magistrates have power to remand in custody or on bail in these cases.

---

[76] E.g. Ormrod L.J. in Horner v. Horner [1982] Fam. 90, 93, who held that any automatic enforcement of the court's orders was to be deprecated where cases of idiosyncratic behaviour required both sensitive and firm handling.

[77] See para. 5.10 above.

[78] See para. 5.12-5.13 above.

6.41   To give similar powers to county courts and the High Court to remand alleged contemnors in custody or on bail in such cases would be a considerable innovation for which they may not in practice be equipped. Magistrates' courts, after all, are principally criminal courts with the facilities appropriate to such powers. Nevertheless, it may be in the interests of either side that the committal proceedings are adjourned, and on occasions it may be necessary to give interim protection to an applicant who is in imminent danger of physical violence. The apparent disregard of the court's authority should in principle be enough to justify the court in taking control over the future conduct of the contempt proceedings.

(d)   Arrest warrants

6.42   A further difference between the two courts is that, where no power of arrest has been attached, an applicant for any order in a magistrates' court can obtain an arrest warrant for breach of the order, and once arrested, the respondent can be remanded in custody on bail until enforcement proceedings are determined.[79] To provide such a power in other courts would be an even greater innovation than the existing power of arrest.

(e)   New enforcement powers

6.43   One possible solution would be to give magistrates' courts power to enforce injunctions granted in higher courts, rather as they can enforce maintenance orders at present. A further solution would be to make breach of certain orders a criminal offence to be prosecuted in the normal way. Of course, the same behaviour may constitute both a breach of the order and a criminal offence and the alternative of prosecution should be in the minds of both applicant and police. Nevertheless, when the Scottish Law Commission considered

---

[79] See para. 5.8 above.

this suggestion, they concluded that it was important that the enforcement of an interdict should remain under the control of the court which had granted it and which (in theory at least) was aware of all the facts and circumstances.[80] They further believed that there were considerable advantages in retaining the civil courts' "flexible and speedy" powers to deal with breaches, avoiding the need for a criminal trial, yet securing the involvement of the police, and the arrest and detention of the respondent at least for a short while.[81] The main complaint in this country is not that powers of arrest exist at all, but that courts appear reluctant to attach them, the police are sometimes reluctant to implement them, and the powers available to the court following arrest are defective.[82]

(v)   Emergency procedures

6.44   Civil procedures have been criticised as being "cumbersome, lengthy and subject to many delays".[83] One reason could be reluctance to grant ex parte relief. It is always difficult to balance the need to allow an applicant to pursue her remedy in peace and safety against the need to allow the respondent an opportunity of putting his side of the case. The present guidelines for ex parte orders[84] could draw a clearer distinction between orders against molestation, which do not

---

80. Report on Occupancy Rights in the Matrimonial Home and Domestic Violence (1980), Scot. Law Com. No.60, para. 4.34.

81. Ibid., para.4.35.

82. T. Faraghar,"The police response to violence against women in the home" and S. Parker, "The legal background" in J. Pahl (ed.) Private Violence and Public Policy (1985); London Strategic Policy Unit, Police Response to Domestic Violence (1986); S. Edwards, The Police Response to Domestic Violence in London (1986) Central London Polytechnic; S. Parsloe, "Battered by men and bruised by the law", (1987) The Law Magazine, 4 Sept.

83. See L. Smith, Domestic Violence: an overview of the literature (1989), Home Office Research Study No. 107, p.90.

84. Para. 5.2 above.

harm the respondent's interests, and ouster orders, which do. Secondly, the criteria in the higher courts, requiring a "real immediate danger of serious injury or irreparable harm" are more severe than those for an expedited order in a magistrates' court which require "imminent danger of physical injury".[85] Thirdly, even where it is difficult to show such danger, there may be evidence that the respondent has deliberately evaded service. The guidance given might be revised to reflect some or all of these concerns.

6.45   Finally, magistrates' courts might be empowered to grant expedited exclusion orders as well as personal protection orders. Expedited orders must always be approached with great caution but, once again, the issues are not intrinsically more difficult, or the consequences more serious, than many other decisions which are open to magistrates at present.

(2)   A new structure

6.46   Family law essentially consists of a collection of largely discretionary remedies to meet particular problems arising in family life.   Where new remedies are devised to meet newly recognised problems, as with the Matrimonial Homes Act and the Domestic Violence Act, there is always a risk that inconsistencies will develop.   Where particular remedies are devised for use in magistrates' courts, the inconsistency may be deliberate.   Nevertheless, the aim of the Commission's work in family law has been to devise simple, clear and consistent remedies available so far as possible in all courts having jurisdiction in family matters.[86] The position which has developed in relation to civil remedies against domestic violence or molestation and the occupation of the family home is neither simple, clear nor

---

85. See paras. 5.2-5.5 above.

86. This was the principal aim of the review of child law culminating in the Children Bill now before Parliament.

consistent. We should prefer to see a unified structure if one can be devised.

6.47   The scheme which is outlined below builds upon the individual reforms discussed earlier to provide an illustration of how a unified structure of remedies might look. It does not depend, however, upon acceptance of each and every one of its constituent parts. It would, for example, be simple to retain the present criteria for ouster and occupation orders within such a basic structure. We ourselves have not reached any provisional conclusions about the individual reforms, upon which we would welcome views, as well as on the structure outlined below.

(i)   The orders available

6.48   The court might have power to make one or more of the following orders, in substance the same as those which may currently be made in the higher courts:[87]

(a) prohibiting one party from molesting the other;

(b) prohibiting one party from molesting a child;

(c) requiring one party to leave the home;

(d) prohibiting one party from entering or re-entering the home, or part of the home, or a defined area in which the home is included;

(e) requiring one party to allow the other to enter and remain in the home;

[87.] In proceedings under the 1976 or 1983 Acts or ancillary to divorce or other family proceedings.

91

(f) regulating the occupation of the home by either or both of the parties.

6.49   The following ancillary powers might also be provided:

(a) to grant one party the possession or use of some or all of the furnishings and other contents of the home;

(b) to make conditions and exceptions (for example, as to visiting the children or collecting clothing or permitting children to enter the home with the applicant);

(c) to impose on either party obligations as to the repair and maintenance of the home or the discharge of outgoings in respect of it;

(d) to order the party occupying the home to make periodical payments to the other in respect of that occupation; this might be restricted to cases where the party occupying did so otherwise than by virtue of a legal or beneficial right to do so or extended to cases where both parties were so entitled.

(ii)   Rights of occupation

6.50   The present statutory rights of spouses to occupy the matrimonial home would remain.[88] Where only one spouse is legally entitled to the home it would be necessary to preserve the court's power to bring to an end the rights of occupation of the non-entitled spouse.[89] This is principally to deal with the deadlocks which can

---

88. See para. 2.5 above.

89. Matrimonial Homes Act 1983, s.1(2)(a).

92

result from the registration of occupation rights to protect against dispositions to third parties. The spouse's right to register such rights would also remain as it is at present.

6.51   Where a person who is not a spouse and is not legally entitled to the home[90] obtains an order allowing him or her to enter or remain there, the effect of such an order could be, as it is in Scotland, to grant short term occupation rights.[91]   These would be equivalent to those of a spouse as against the other party. However, we would not suggest that they should be a charge upon the property itself and thus capable of being protected, whether by registration, or otherwise, against dispositions to third parties.

(iii)   Transfer of tenancies

6.52   The power to transfer protected, statutory, secure and assured tenancies from one spouse to another (or from joint names to one of them)[92] on or after divorce would also remain as it is at present. As previously discussed,[93] if there is to be power to regulate rights of occupation between certain non-spouses, there would also be advantages for all concerned in giving similar powers to transfer the tenancy itself.

---

90. For the persons who might be entitled to apply for the orders proposed in para. 6.48 see para. 6.56 below.

91. See para. 6.5 above.

92. Matrimonial Homes Act 1983, s.7 and sched.1; see para. 2.5 above.

93. At para. 6.6 above.

(iv)   Effect on third party rights

6.53   The above suggestions would effect only minor changes in the
present position of third parties such as prior mortgagees or
landlords, purchasers and subsequent mortgagees.   Where spouses are
concerned, their position would remain exactly as it is at present.   A
power to regulate occupation rights between jointly entitled
non-spouses would place the landlord or prior mortgagee in no worse
position than he is at present, because both would remain liable for
the rent or mortgage instalments.   A power to grant short-term
occupation rights to a non-entitled non-spouse is in effect already
available by virtue of the House of Lords' decision in Davis v.
Johnson[94] and these proposals would simply spell out the consequences
of that.   The landlord or prior mortgagee would be in no worse, but
also no better, position than if the original occupant had remained in
sole occupation.   In particular, if the original occupant had no
security of tenure it would always be open to the landlord to bring
the tenancy or licence to an end.   A power to transfer protected,
statutory, secure or assured tenancies would, of course, be a
considerable change, but the landlord would be entitled to voice his
objections to such a transfer and might welcome the court's power to
resolve the deadlock which can otherwise arise where the relationship
between tenants with security of tenure breaks down.[95]   It is not
suggested that any new land charge be created, and so the position of
prospective purchasers or subsequent mortgagees will be unaffected by
these proposals.

---

94. [1979] A.C. 264; para. 2.12 above.

95. See para. 4.9, 6.6 and 6.12 above.

(v)   <u>Proceedings in which orders may be made</u>

6.54   In the same way that the Children Bill provides for the circumstances in which the courts' powers to make orders arise,[96] it could be made clear that orders may be made:

> (a) on application (by a person entitled so to do) without any other proceedings being instituted; or

> (b) on application (by a person entitled so to do) in the course of any family proceedings.

It would be advantageous to define "family proceedings" in the same way as they are defined in the Children Bill.[97] This would enable all cases concerning the same family to be heard together. It would also facilitate the introduction of a common jurisdictional scheme enabling transfer of cases within the system along the same lines as that intended to implement the Children Bill.[98]

6.55   The Children Bill also provides for most orders to be made of the court's own motion as well as on application,[99] but that may be thought less appropriate to orders regulating the lives of adults than

---

[96.] Clause 9(1) and (2).

[97.] Defined in clause 7(3) and (4) as any proceedings under the inherent jurisdiction of the High Court in relation to children or under Parts I, II and IV of the Bill itself, the Matrimonial Causes Act 1973, the Domestic Violence and Matrimonial Proceedings Act 1976, the Adoption Act 1976, the Domestic Proceedings and Magistrates' Courts Act 1978, ss.1 and 9 of the Matrimonial Homes Act 1923, and Part III of the Matrimonial and Family Proceedings Act 1984.

[98.] Under clause 82.

[99.] Clause 9(1)(b).

it is for orders relating to children where the court may have to make immediate provision for their care or upbringing and has traditionally not been restricted to the orders sought by the parties to the case.[100].

(vi)   Adult parties

6.56   The present system provides essentially for remedies between two adults who are related in a defined way.   It is necessary to prescribe not only who may be an applicant but also who may be a respondent. Remedies might be made available between:

(a) spouses; i.e. a man and woman who are married to one another;

(b) former spouses;

(c) cohabitants; i.e. a man and woman who are living with each other as husband and wife in the same household;

(d) former cohabitants; and possibly

(e) parents or others having parental responsibility for a child within the meaning of the Children Bill; i.e. any guardian, and any other person with the benefit of a residence order under the Bill.[101]

---

100. See e.g. Re E. (S.A.)(A Minor)(Wardship) [1984] 1 W.L.R. 156, (H.L.).

101. Clauses 5(5) and 11(2); local authorities will also acquire parental responsibility for children under care orders, clause 28(3).

6.57   All these categories would be able to apply for protection against molestation (orders (a) and (b)). Spouses would be able to apply for all orders. Otherwise, entitlement to apply for ouster and other occupation related remedies might be limited by reference to his or her entitlement to occupy the premises under the general law. Thus:

(a) a person with a legal, beneficial or statutory right to occupy could always apply, whether or not the other person was so entitled; but

(b) a person with no legal, or beneficial or statutory right to occupy could only apply within a certain period of the divorce or ending of the relationship (and, as we shall see in the next paragraph, only for short term relief); and

(c) a parent with no such right could not apply at all (because the premises would never have been the family home).

The period prescribed in (b) might be until the determination of any application for a transfer of propety or transfer of tenancy order or the expiry of a fixed period, which could be related to the potential duration of orders in such cases.

(vii)   Duration of orders

6.58   All orders would be capable of being made for a specified period (or until a specified event) or until further order. However, orders relating to occupation made for the benefit of a person with no legal, beneficial or statutory right to occupy might be limited in duration, perhaps on the Scottish model[102] to three months in the first instance with renewal thereafter for periods of up to six months at a time, or perhaps more limited, for example to one renewal for up

---

102. Matrimonial Homes (Family Protection)(Scotland) Act 1987, s.18(1).

to a further three months or to a total (however many orders were involved) of six months.

(viii) Children protected

6.59   This could extend to any child who was the child of either party or living with either party. As already indicated, parties could include people with the benefit of a residence order under the Children Bill. To go further would be to allow unrelated adults to interfere in the lives of children by applying for orders about them without having any responsibility for their upbringing or complying with the qualifications and safeguards in the Children Bill.[103] However, a possible scheme for local authorities to apply to protect children by means of such orders is discussed in Appendix A.

(ix)   Criteria for orders

6.60   All orders would be discretionary and the generally applicable criterion would be, as it is at present, what is fair, just and reasonable in all the circumstances of the case. The relevant considerations in exercising that discretion might be modified in the light of the earlier discussions,[104] perhaps as follows.

6.61   In relation to molestation orders, the court might be permitted to make such order as in all the circumstances is fair, just and reasonable in the interests of the health, safety or well-being of the applicant or child concerned.

---

103. See clause 9(4)-(9).

104. See paras. 6.24-6.34, also para. 3.8 et seq.

6.62   In relation to occupation orders, the court might be directed to apply the "balance of hardship" test, by making such order as in all the circumstances is fair, just and reasonable, in the light of:

(a) whether the parties can reasonably be expected to live or continue to live under the same roof;

(b) the parties' respective needs and resources, in particular the hardship caused to each party if the order is made or not made; and

(c) the welfare of any child concerned, which should be considered both in its own right and in relation to factors (a) and (b) above.

6.63   This formulation of the child's welfare is suggested in order to indicate to the court its relevance to each of the other factors. It would not be paramount, in the sense that it would prevail no matter how reasonable it was to expect the parties to stay in the same house or how great the hardship involved, but if brought into account at each stage of the process, it would achieve a greater importancee than it has at present under the Matrimonial Homes Act. This might also give a clearer indication of its relative weight than would referring to it as the "first" consideration.[105]   It would also be possible to strengthen these criteria with a requirement that, if violence (or some form of it) were shown, greater weight should be given to the protection of the victim (whether applicant or child).

(x)   Enforcement

6.64   The court might be enabled to attach a power of arrest to any order, provided:

[105.] See para. 6.32 above.

(a) that the respondent had in fact caused actual bodily harm to the victim (whether applicant or child); and

(b) that the order specified exactly which breaches of the order would give rise to the power of arrest;

unless in all the circumstances it appears that the applicant or child will be adequately protected without it.

6.65   After arrest, any court could have power to remand the person arrested, either in custody or on bail, pending proceedings for committal or breach.

(xi)   Ex parte orders

6.66   The courts might be given power to make orders ex parte where there is imminent danger of actual bodily harm to the applicant or child if the order is not made immediately, or where every effort has been made to effect service and there is reason to believe that the respondent is evading it.

(xii)   Magistrates' courts

6.67   It would be possible to limit the powers of magistrates within such a structure in a number of ways:

(a) by limiting the adult parties involved, for example to married couples;

(b) by limiting the orders available, for example excluding wider forms of anti-molestation or transfer of tenancy orders;

(c) by limiting the grounds, for example to cases of actual or threatened violence.

The only essential limitation, however, might be to require them to transfer the case (were this to be possible under the new scheme) or to refuse jurisdiction, if a dispute arose as to whether or not either party had a legal, beneficial or statutory right to occupy the home.

Conclusion

6.68   Although we have canvassed many individual reforms and two overall approaches to reform, we are conscious of the view of at least one commentator[106] that the law already provides adequate remedies in this field, and of others that "where the legal system really fails is in the application, operation and interpretation of legislative provisions."[107] The object of the reforms discussed here is not to make fundamental change in the existing system.   It is, first, to propose amendments which might assist in improving the application, operation and interpretation of the present procedure, and secondly, to remove the gaps, anomalies and inconsistencies between the different provisions.   We should however welcome views upon whether there is a need to effect real improvements in practice, and if so how far this can be done through law reforms of the sort discussed here, as well as on the possible reforms themselves.[108]

---

106. S. Maidment, "Domestic violence and the law: the 1976 Act and its aftermath" in N. Johnson (ed.) Marital Violence (1985).

107. Smith, op. cit., p.34.

108. A checklist of the particular questions raised in the first part of Part VI appears as Appendix B.

APPENDIX A

OUSTER ORDERS FOR THE PROTECTION OF CHILDREN

1.   Present private law remedies offer only indirect protection
against child abuse, as orders may only be obtained by one adult
against another, and indeed only certain categories of adults, who may
not include every member of the child's household. Further, the
criteria do not give priority to the need to protect the child from
harm. During the passage of the Children Bill through Parliament,
considerable support was given to the possibility of ousting an abuser
or suspected abuser from the home instead of having to remove the
child.[1] In practice, this possibility would only be an effective
protection against child abuse in a relatively small proportion of
cases.[2] The abuse must be of a kind for which only one of the adults
(usually a father or step-father) in the household is responsible.
There must be another adult (usually the mother) who is able to look
after the child properly and also willing to co-operate in the
exclusion of the other. Further, there would not be the same need for
a remedy of this sort in cases which were not serious enough to
warrant the removal of the child from home. Several methods of
providing an ouster power in such cases could be envisaged but none is
without difficulty. The discussion which follows assumes the
enactment and implementation of the Children Bill now before
Parliament.

---

[1]. Official Report (H.C.), Standing Committee B, 25 May 1989, cols.
325-329.

[2]. Child abuse covers all types of neglect or ill-treatment, physical,
sexual or emotional, but the possibility of ousting the suspected
abuser is probably most relevant in cases of sexual abuse or
serious "one-off" incidents of violence.

(i)   Hearing care and private law proceedings together

2.   One possibility would be to consolidate the local authority's application for a care, supervision or emergency protection order,[3] with the mother's application for ouster or protection against violence or molestation, thus permitting the court to choose between them. The Children Bill goes some way towards providing for this, in that applications for care and supervision orders may be made in the course of any family proceedings, including those under the Matrimonial Homes Act 1983, Domestic Violence and Matrimonial Proceedings Act 1976 and Domestic Proceedings and Magistrates' Courts Act 1978.[4] It does not, however, provide for the reverse situation, in which applications under those provisions may be made in the course of care proceedings. This would no doubt be helpful, but it would not provide the court with any alternative or additional powers where an emergency protection order was sought, and would continue to place the burden of seeking the order upon the parent who hoped to retain the child.

(ii)   Allowing local authority applications for private law remedies

3.   A further possibility might therefore be to allow local authorities to apply for the private law remedies discussed in the working paper. This should presumably be limited to cases where there is a risk of harm to the child, as this is the general criterion under which local authorities have power to initiate compulsory intervention in family life.[5] It might also be desirable to limit the power to cases where the parent looking after the child either

---

[3.] Under clauses 28(1) and 38(1).

[4.] See clauses 28(4) and 7(3) and (4).

[5.] Incorporated in the criteria for care and supervision orders (clause 28(2)); emergency protection orders (clause 38(1)); and granting leave to a local authority to invoke the wardship or other inherent jurisdiction of the court (clause 84(4)).

requested or at least consented to the application. Without her cooperation, the order is unlikely to provide any protection for the child. Further, unless the existing criteria are revised to give greater weight to the protection of the child from abuse, the authority may find that an ouster order is more difficult to obtain than a care order. In practice, therefore, the authority would probably wish to bring care proceedings at the same time, so that alternative methods of protecting the child were available if ouster or non-molestation remedies proved inadequate.

(iii) Accepting undertakings in emergency protection cases

4.   During the passage of the Children Bill through Parliament, amendments were moved to permit the court, instead of making an emergency protection order, to accept a voluntary undertaking to leave the home or sever contact with the child.[6] There are obvious attractions in providing for the court to accept the offer of a solution which will allow the child to remain undisturbed in the home for a relatively short period while further investigations are made. However, applications for emergency protection orders will generally be made ex parte, and the proceedings would therefore have to be adjourned in order to arrange for the people concerned to attend. This would be dangerous for the child if it was a genuine emergency where the grounds for making an emergency protection order appeared satisfied at the initial hearing. Further, enforcement of an undertaking is slow and at present no power of arrest can be attached. If, as was the case with the amendments discussed in Parliament, no emergency protection order could be made once such an undertaking had been accepted, then the child might not be properly protected. If, on the other hand, such an undertaking were to be combined with an emergency protection order, little advantage would be gained over the existing provisions in the Bill. These already insist that the child must not be removed or kept away from home under the order if it is

---

[6.] See n.1 above.

safe for him to return.[7] The applicant for an emergency protection order can therefore accept a voluntary undertaking to leave and return the child once it has been honoured. Further, the parent looking after the child at home will have little incentive to report a breach of the undertaking if the only real sanction is the instant removal of the child.

(iv) Ouster and non-molestation orders in care, etc. proceedings

5.   Some of these disadvantages could be avoided by giving the court, in proceedings for emergency protection, care or supervision orders under the Bill, power to order a member of the child's household to leave, together if need be with orders restraining contact or molestation. The criteria and effects could be directly related to the criteria and effects applicable at the stage which the care proceedings had reached.

6.   Thus, for example, the main ground for an emergency protection order is that there is reasonable cause to believe that the child is likely to suffer significant harm if not removed or kept away from home.[8] The additional ground for ouster in such cases could be reasonable cause to believe that harm will not occur provided that the person concerned is excluded from the home. Emergency protection orders last for up to eight days, but may be extended for up to seven days more where care proceedings are under contemplation but the applicant is not yet ready to proceed.[9] For such a short period, no further criteria may be needed.

[7.] Clause 36(7).

[8.] Clause 36(1)(a).

[9.] Clause 37(1)-(6).

7.   If care proceedings are brought, interim care or supervision orders may be made if there are reasonable grounds for believing that the minimum conditions for the order exist, i.e. (a) that the child is suffering or is likely to suffer significant harm and (b) that this is because he is not receiving, or likely to receive a reasonable standard of parental care or he is beyond parental control.[10] Once again, the additional criterion for ouster at the interim stage might therefore be that there are reasonable grounds for believing that the child will not suffer significant harm if the person concerned is excluded from the home. Interim orders are of limited duration, so that again it may be unnecessary to provide further criteria, given that the order will in any event be discretionary.

8.   The Children Bill also provides that where a court determines any question with respect to the upbringing (including the care) of a child, the child's welfare shall be the paramount consideration.[11] Unless this principle is also applied to the question of ouster in these short term cases, the court will not in effect be able to choose which solution will be best for the child. Even if it were plain that the child would be much better off at home, the court would have to balance this against the interests of the adults concerned. On the other hand, the hardship to the adult concerned (against whom nothing might yet have been proved) could be considerable. This would be mitigated if local authorites had power, as part of the services provided to prevent child abuse[12] to offer him accommodation during this period.

9.   Should such an order be made along with an emergency protection or interim care order or as an alternative to it? The

---

10. Clauses 33(2) and 26(2).

11. Clause 1(1).

12. Schedule 2, para.4.

former would allow the local authority to remove the child at any time if there was a suspicion that the person ousted had returned. However, unless provision were made to the contrary, it would also allow removal even if he did not return, which would mean that the family lost both ways. If removal were only to be possible for breach of the ouster order, then the authority should in principle be required to show this, albeit if necessary ex parte, before taking action. It might be preferable, therefore, to provide for ouster as an alternative to emergency protection or interim care. Given that the criteria for these had already been proved, it would be relatively simple to seek a variation should the need arise. In an interim care case, at least, the ouster order could also be combined with an interim supervision order, which would give the authority access to monitor the position.

10.   If the courts had power to make such orders, they would also be able to make them by consent, or accept undertakings in the same way that they do at present. The attractions of these orders as an alternative to removing the child would be greatly increased if a power of arrest could be attached. At present, powers of arrest cannot be attached to undertakings at all, or to orders unless harm has actually been proved. It would be a considerable innovation to allow either, but might be thought justifiable in the short term if it would increase confidence in a remedy which is designed to protect a child from the trauma and stigma of a sudden removal from his home, family and friends.

11.   Such measures may be contemplated for short periods, but could they be justified as an alternative to a full care order? It would seem strange if the court were able to oust a suspected but not a proven abuser. However, if long term ouster were contemplated, the court would presumably have to consider the respective property and occupation rights of the adult parties and, in cases where the person ousted had rights of occupation, the balance of hardship between them. Further, whereas interim protection might be granted against any

member of the child's household, longer term remedies might have to depend upon the general law of property or family relationships. If so, at this stage, it might be preferable to allow the private law remedies to be granted in the care proceedings rather than to continue to provide a separate scheme. The solution is unlikely to commend itself to the court in the long term unless it has the whole-hearted support of the parent with whom the child is to remain. Indeed, without that support the effect, at least between married parties, could be akin to an imposed divorce or at least judicial separation. Such an interference in family life might be thought to be in breach of the European Convention on Human Rights[13] even if the overriding purpose were the protection of a child.

---

13. Article 8(1).

In Part VI we identified two broad categories for reform. The first
raises quite specific proposals relating to the persons protected, the
scope and duration of remedies, criteria for orders, powers of arrest
and emergency procedures. These proposals in themselves provide a
necessary part of the context of the more comprehensive reform set out
in the second part of Part VI. The questions below are designed to
focus attention on the particular questions raised by the discussion
in the first part of Part VI.

Question 1

What (if any) improvements might be made in the
statutory criteria with respect to:

a) personal protection orders?
   [paras. 6.25-6.26]

b) ouster orders? [paras. 6.25, 6.27-6.33]

c) the regulation of occupation rights?
   [paras. 6.7, 6.25, 6.27-6.33]

Question 2

Should statute define and if so in what way:

a) the criteria for non-molestation orders?
   [para. 6.26]

b) molestation itself? [para. 6.15-6.16]

Question 3

To what extent should the court have power to
grant molestation and occupation remedies to:

a) former spouses? [para. 6.2]

b) former cohabitants? [para. 6.3]

Question 4

Should occupation remedies granted to non-entitled non-spouses have the same effect (as against the other party) as a spouse's rights of occupation under the Matrimonial Homes Act 1983? [para. 6.4]

Question 5

Should there be power to transfer tenancies with statutory security of tenure between cohabitants? [para. 6.6]

Question 6

Should there be power to determine property disputes between cohabitants under section 17 of the Married Women's Property Act 1882? [para. 6.9]

Question 7

Should there be power to regulate rights of occupation between parties who have obtained a joint tenancy on the basis of shared parental responsibility but who have never lived together as husband and wife?   [para. 6.12]

Question 8

Should magistrates' courts be enabled to:
a)   grant personal protection orders and exclusion orders to cohabitants? [paras. 6.8, 6.22]
b)   prohibit molestation?
     [paras. 6.16, 6.33, 6.42]
c)   regulate, enforce or grant rights of occupation? [paras. 6.21-6.22, 6.34]

Question 9

Should there be power in all proceedings to:

a) exclude the respondent from a specified area in which the home is situated or from part only of the home? [para. 6.17]

b) make ancillary orders as to the discharge of rent, mortgage instalments or other outgoings? [paras. 6.5, 6.18-6.19]

Question 10

Should there be a power in all proceedings to make orders about the use of furniture? [para. 6.20]

Question 11

Should guidelines on the duration of ouster orders be revised? [para. 6.23]

Question 12

Should there be a statutory time limit for occupation orders granted to non-entitled non-spouses? [paras. 6.5, 6.24]

Question 13

Which children should be protected by non-molestation and personal protection orders? [para. 6.11]

Question 14

Should standing to apply for non-molestation and ouster orders be extended to:

a) local authorities for the protection of children who are at risk of abuse? [para 6.13 and Appendix A]

b) the police, (or others) on the victim's behalf? [para 6.14]

Question 15

Are the criteria for powers of arrest satisfactory? [para. 6.38-6.39]]

Question 16

Should the scope of orders to which a power of arrest may be attached be extended to:
a) cover former spouses and cohabitants? [para 6.2-6.3, 6.37]
b) orders granted under the Matrimonial Homes Act 1983 Act? [para 6.36]
c) similar orders in all family proceedings? [para. 6.37]

Question 17

Should the High Court and county courts have power to:
a) remand a respondent who has been arrested under a power of arrest either in custody or on bail? [paras. 6.40-6.41]
b) grant an arrest warrant for breach of the court's orders? [para. 6.42]

Question 18

Should magistrates' courts be enabled to enforce injunctions granted in the higher courts? [para. 6.43]

Question 19

Should guidelines on ex parte orders be revised? [para. 6.44]

Question 20

Should magistrates' courts be enabled to grant expedited exclusion orders? [para. 6.45]

Printed in the United Kingdom for Her Majesty's Stationery Office.
Dd.0291272, 8/89, C15, 3390/3, 5673, 70854.